"This is a very fine, well wr[...]
start well, do well, and fini[...]
commend it to our students[...]

—DANIEL L. AKIN, PRESIDENT, SOUTHEASTERN BAPTIST
THEOLOGICAL SEMINARY (WAKE FOREST, NC)

"Theological education ought to be a season of tremendous intellectual and spiritual growth for the students who undertake it. Unfortunately, this is not always the case. Too many seminarians find themselves overwhelmed by classroom responsibilities, family commitments, and financial challenges. That is why every seminary student would be wise to read *Surviving and Thriving in Seminary* by Benjamin Forrest and Daniel Zacharias. As the title indicates, this book will be an essential tool for all pursuing theological education, and for all who desire to graduate and look back joyously on their season of ministry training."

—JASON K. ALLEN, PRESIDENT, MIDWESTERN BAPTIST
THEOLOGICAL SEMINARY (KANSAS CITY, MO)

"Daniel Zacharias and Benjamin Forrest have written an immensely helpful book on how to prepare yourself when you're totally unprepared for seminary. If you're starting seminary, this book will give you a head start, and hopefully prevent you from turning your Christian life into a train wreck. This book covers everything you should know from prayer life to research skills to time management. I wish someone had told me this when I went to seminary."

—MICHAEL F. BIRD, LECTURER IN THEOLOGY, RIDLEY
COLLEGE (MELBOURNE, AUSTRALIA)

"Surviving in seminary is a worthy quest, but it is inconsequential compared to thriving in seminary. Zacharias and Forrest have written a book that I wish I had had the foresight to write. Every student headed to a seminary or divinity school ought to read this book carefully before undertaking the journey. Chapter two on preparing your heart and chapter 5 on managing your time" are 100 percent worth the price of the book. Read this book and then enjoy your seminary journey."

—PAIGE PATTERSON, PRESIDENT, SOUTHWESTERN BAPTIST
THEOLOGICAL SEMINARY (FORT WORTH, TX)

"*Surviving and Thriving in Seminary* is essential reading for the next generation of seminary students. In this carefully designed book, Forrest and Zacharias, with much wisdom and pastoral guidance, have thoughtfully introduced their readers to the multiple aspects of theological education, including shaping minds, transforming lives, as well as forming men and women for ministry. The authors have presented students with a great gift, providing both current and prospective students, as well as their families, with a thorough overview of the realities, privileges, blessings, responsibilities, and challenges involved in pursuing seminary education. Forrest and Zacharias are to be congratulated on producing this extremely helpful and beneficial volume."

—DAVID S. DOCKERY, PRESIDENT, TRINITY EVANGELICAL
DIVINITY SCHOOL (DEERFIELD, IL)

"Wise leaders know that the first person one must lead is oneself. The authors of *Surviving and Thriving in Seminary* offer godly wisdom and practical counsel in doing just that when it comes to preparing for and engaging the seminary experience. Out of their own life and educational experiences, the authors provide a fast-paced orientation that is inviting, direct and helpful. Overall, the message is clear. Take responsibility for your life as a student and here are some very practical tools to do so. Whether that responsibility is for your spiritual life, being sensitive to your friends or family's needs, or writing an excellent assignment, you will find some of the clearest guidelines and resources provided here. I strongly recommend the book to students as well as seminaries who want to prepare students well!"

—HARRY GARDNER, PRESIDENT, ACADIA DIVINITY COLLEGE;
DEAN OF THEOLOGY, ACADIA UNIVERSITY (WOLFVILLE, NS)

"A manual of practical and spiritual wisdom for every seminary student—and for those who are thinking about becoming one. Highly recommended!"

—TIMOTHY GEORGE, FOUNDING DEAN OF BEESON DIVINITY
SCHOOL OF SAMFORD UNIVERSITY (BIRMINGHAM, AL); GENERAL
EDITOR OF THE REFORMATION COMMENTARY ON SCRIPTURE

"Attending seminary is an experience that is both challenging and rewarding. Daniel Zacharias and Benjamin Forrest have written this book to guide seminarians through those challenges and get the most out of their seminary experience. Whether you are a young seminarian who is able to devote all of your time to attending classes and studying or are struggling to keep your sanity while juggling the responsibilities of seminary, family, and job, you will find this book immensely helpful!"

—Michael R. Licona, associate professor of theology, Houston Baptist University (Houston, TX)

"This very helpful book fills a real void. Studying at seminary is a wonderful opportunity, but it is also a challenge. Prospective students can now draw on the wealth of practical advice offered by Forrest and Zacharias. It will enable them to make wise choices and get the most out of their seminary experience. The book is rooted in a North American context, but there is much on these pages that will also benefit students in other parts of the world. Highly recommended."

—Peter J. Morden, vice principal, Spurgeon's College (London, England)

"*Surviving and Thriving in Seminary* is pure gold. In it, Benjamin Forrest and Daniel Zacharias coach prospective and beginning seminary students on how to get the most out of their seminary experience. They show why seminary students—in all of their striving to learn—should work hard to realize the importance of oft-neglected realities such as the biblical languages, personal spiritual formation, healthy holistic lifestyles, financial planning, and caring for one's family. If you are a prospective or beginning seminary student, this little book might make all the difference for you."

—Bruce Ashford, provost and professor of theology and culture, Southeastern Baptist Theological Seminary (Wake Forest, NC)

"Forrest and Zacharias thoughtfully integrate biblical wisdom with both their own experience as students and their observations as professors to provide seminarians with a wonderful guide on how to navigate theological education in a manner that optimizes its benefits. Compared to similar books on this topic, this one is especially valuable because of the attention given to family dynamics and its helpful suggestions on how to use contemporary tools for organizing one's life and learning."

—RANDAL ROBERTS, PRESIDENT AND PROFESSOR OF CHRISTIAN SPIRITUALITY, WESTERN SEMINARY (PORTLAND, OR)

Surviving

and

Thriving

in

Seminary

Surviving *and* Thriving *in* Seminary

An Academic and
Spiritual Handbook

H. Daniel Zacharias
and Benjamin K. Forrest

LEXHAM PRESS

Surviving and Thriving in Seminary: An Academic and Spiritual Handbook

Copyright 2017 H. Daniel Zacharias and Benjamin K. Forrest

Lexham Press, 1313 Commercial St., Bellingham, WA 98225
LexhamPress.com

Print ISBN 978-1-57-799778-8
Digital ISBN 978-1-57-799779-5

Lexham Editorial Team: Elliot Ritzema, Jennifer Edwards
Cover Design: Bryan Hintz
Back Cover Design: Liz Donovan
Typesetting: ProjectLuz.com

Contents

Introduction

This is a no-nonsense guide to success in seminary. We are not going to teach you theology or give you an introduction to biblical studies; that is what your courses will do. Instead, we want to talk to you about things that should be covered in every seminary orientation. We want not only to help you understand the reality of what you are getting yourself into, but also to equip you with the skills to succeed—spiritually, relationally, and academically.

Students attend seminary for many reasons. You may be pursuing vocational ministry. You may want to go on to doctoral studies. Or you may just be taking courses, residentially or online, out of interest and a desire for growth. While we all have our own particular goals, we believe there are certain skills and habits that apply to anyone in a seminary context. So whether you are on the cusp of entering seminary, you are already there (perhaps you have become frustrated with your experience), or your professor assigned this as introductory reading in one of your first seminary courses, we believe that this book can help encourage and give you the skills you need to survive and thrive.

WHAT MAKES THIS BOOK UNIQUE?

Perhaps it is the information age, perhaps it is our society that likes everything instantaneously, or perhaps it is our own impatience, but we don't like long, drawn-out writing. What you'll find here is concise, practical advice. This book is written in a conversational style and short enough to read through in one or two evenings. We're not going to mince words, go into long speeches, or provide comprehensive theological justifications for things that are founded in Scripture (like the fact that if you're a parent you still need to parent while you're a seminary student!).

We're also not going to coddle you or pull any punches. We know *exactly* how students sabotage themselves and procrastinate because we've done it and seen it done. Being a seminary student is rewarding, but it is also demanding. You need to know this ahead of time so you are not blindsided.

Throughout, we provide numerous recommendations for apps and other tools to help you study and manage your time. However, remember that not all people will find the same tool equally helpful, and since technology moves fast, new tools are always coming out. Please take the time to evaluate and decide for yourself what solution is right for you.

While most of our writing comes from the collective "we," occasionally we have felt the need when telling personal stories to clarify which one of us is speaking by putting "Danny" or "Ben" in parentheses.

WHY LISTEN TO US?

These days anyone can write a book regardless of their knowledge or experience. Still, we hope you listen to us for these reasons:

Danny has completed a BA, an MDiv, an MA in theology, and a PhD in New Testament studies. He's been in post-secondary theological education longer than he was in grade school (it hurts to admit that!). He completed the last three of his degrees while he also had a growing family. He was actively involved in lay ministry or in a part-time pastoral position through most of those degree programs. After earning two degrees in a seminary, he now works full time as a seminary professor. He was a D student in high school—but he crushed it in seminary.

Ben started college as an education major. After graduating, he completed an MA in religion and a master's in religious education. Following seminary, he completed an EdS and an EdD. His dissertation research focused on the spiritually formative experiences of seminary spouses. His passion and research coalesce in this topic: thriving in seminary! This passion, however, is not just for the thriving of seminary students, but their families as well. Like Danny, Ben was eventually hired as a professor at the seminary he attended. Now that he is a full-time faculty member, he is daily reminded of the challenges, joys, and potential for the seminary experience, and hopes that *you* experience all that God has for you during this season of your life!

In short, we've been where you are. It was only a few years ago, so it is still fresh in our memories. And now we are in a position not only to look back and see what we could have done better, but to also see the struggles our current students still have. This book is *wisdom from the trenches*.

There are three parts to this book. Part 1 is all about preparation. The most successful people always go in with a plan. Because seminary will occupy a dominant portion of your life, you and those around you need to prepare accordingly. Part 2 covers the practical mechanics of managing your life in the midst of seminary so that you do not burn out. We show you how to take charge of your education and make the best use of your time and energy. Part 3 seeks to equip you with both the skills and tools needed to make the most of your seminary experience.

Here we go!

PART 1

PREPARATION

CHAPTER 1

Preparing Your Mind

Like many seminary students, you may have grown up reading the Bible, attending Sunday school, going to Bible camp, etc. All of these have given you a hunger for God's Word, as well as a desire to serve him and others. This has brought you to seminary, and that is a great thing!

But we have both good news and bad news for you. First the good news: You will learn and understand the Bible in an even deeper way because of the theological training you receive in seminary. But the bad news is that you might not be as prepared as you think you are. Sure, you may know the Bible well, but this does not necessarily mean you are prepared to read and study at an academic level. Even if you have studied the Bible your entire life, you may end up struggling along with everyone else with new terms and concepts that you've never heard before from your pastor or church.

In this chapter, we hope to give you some pointers on how to adjust to the new world of academic, biblical, and theological study you will find in seminary. We will also deal specifically with how you can get ready to study a subject that students often find themselves especially unprepared to tackle: biblical languages.

GET READY FOR DISCOMFORT

Like every field of study, biblical and theological study involves the mastering of new terms and concepts. The difference is your mindset going in. Medical students, for example, go in prepared to learn previously unknown things. You, on the other hand, have likely discussed the Bible and theology with friends and family and listened to speakers talk about it for years. But now you are listening to professors discuss the same subjects in ways you've never heard before. It is jarring and often confusing. Students sometimes rebel, questioning the faith of their professors or wonder why they need to learn "all this new extraneous stuff." If you are tempted to resist new ideas, remind yourself that wisdom and knowledge come from being exposed to and thinking through new ideas—not by refusing to listen or enter into dialogue.

You will not only be faced with new terms and concepts, but these concepts may challenge you on a personal level. Most students in other fields of study take in what they learn from their professors and textbooks with almost total openness. They can do this because what they learn doesn't (usually) challenge them to think differently on a topic that is near and dear to their heart. But in seminary, you are studying things you have previously internalized: the Christian faith, the stories of the Bible, your personal theology, and your ministry future. You meditate on these things; you celebrate them with your faith community, and many of you have already taught and preached on them. The experience of the graduate seminarian is different than those in other fields. Students in music or economics do not generally experience this same relationship with their subject matter prior to their graduate-level studies.

Seminary will ask you to take a step back and look critically at what you believe—not because your professors want to destroy your beliefs, but because they want you to think about whether they are the best way to understand the world, and whether they truly are in line with the Scriptures and not just a folk theology.[1] They want you to expand your thoughts on certain issues. Be willing to entertain another perspective, *even if you do not ultimately agree*. This challenge is great for you—but can at times be a painful process.

Because you will be introduced to new concepts, challenging ideas, and a new way of reading the Scriptures, you need to prepare for discomfort. Sometimes your professor or fellow students will hold a different position than you. While your inclination may be to put up your guard and plug your ears, resist this urge. Discomfort will force you to rethink your position and articulate it better. Or you may change your mind altogether as you come to realize that you held an incorrect or simplistic belief. However, in the midst of discomfort you also need to firmly remind yourself of the fundamentals of orthodox Christian faith. You will very often be challenged on many fronts, but very rarely are students being challenged on

---

1. For a good explanation of our tendency to adopt "folk theologies" see Stanley J. Grenz and Roger E. Olson, *Who Needs Theology?: An Invitation to the Study of God* (Downers Grove, IL: InterVarsity Press, 1996).

the basics. Unless you've chosen to go to a seminary that is extremely different from your own faith tradition, most of your professors will hold to the same fundamental beliefs you do.

When faced with discomfort, it is helpful to remember that there was a process involved in you ending up at the seminary you are now in (or are about to be in).[2] For example, Danny moved across the country to study with a particular professor. Ben, likewise, made a cross-country move. After making such a big decision, it is normal to feel doubt and apprehension. However, if you have thought carefully and sought wise counsel, trust your decision. But recognize that a correct decision does not mean a path that is free of challenges.

Another realm in which many will need to prepare for discomfort is with personal and internal reflection. Seminary is about more than introducing you to the classic disciplines of Bible, theology, and the practice of ministry. It is also about forming you as a person. This means not only continuing to work on your own heart (the subject of the next chapter), but also being mentally prepared to ask hard questions. Although I (Danny) am a biblical scholar and have studied with great people, the most formative points in my seminary journey were not only my New Testament and Greek courses. It was the courses in leadership and counseling that forced me to look at childhood and family issues that shaped some of my negative behaviors and feelings. These were mentally exhausting exercises, and I was often resistant to them because of the mental and emotional energy required. But embrac-

---

2. If you are still in the process of choosing a seminary, we recommend you read appendix 1.

ing the discomfort and diving head first into the work has brought me to the place I am today.

Change is uncomfortable, but discomfort can be good for you. More than that, it is essential if you want to keep growing as a human being. You can be refined into a better person through every trial you face, big or small.

BECOMING THE FUNNEL

Whether you know it or not, what you have learned until you arrive in seminary has gone through a funnel before it reached you. Your pastor, or the preacher whose podcasts you listen to, read books and commentaries to prepare their sermons. They have passed on only a portion to you—the stuff they really wanted you to hear. Your small group leader, Sunday school teacher, or any author of books you have read on Christianity or the Bible have done the same thing. If you read any blogs or visit any Christian websites, they are more than likely sites that those you respect would commonly recommend. And that Christian bookstore you browse and buy books from only carries a handful of publishers—publishers that often don't publish the academic treatises of trained theologians or biblical scholars.

This is why seminary often feels like a whole new world—because it is. In most seminaries, your professors are now teaching you the different opinions on particular

SHARE YOUR THOUGHTS

If you come up with a great idea on how to deal with the new world of seminary as you read this book, please share these ideas with us on Twitter and Facebook using #thrivinginseminary theological positions; they are critiquing ways in which some people have read particular passages of Scripture; they are introducing you to theologians you've never heard of talk about a subject you barely understand; they are asking you to read academic works on these topics you've never considered.

In short, you are now the one being asked to sort through arguments on all sorts of topics and to think through which argument is best and which aligns best with Scripture. *You are now being trained to be the funnel.* It is a daunting and overwhelming task. And it is absolutely worth it!

BE A BUFFALO

Knowing that seminary can be uncomfortable and that you are being trained to be a funnel, you should make the decision to charge right into it with an open mind that is prepared to learn. It is like the difference between cows and buffalo, which Rory Vaden writes about in his book *Take the Stairs*.[3] When cows sense a storm coming, they begin moving away from it. But they are slow, and when the rain is upon them, they keep running *with* the storm! Their attempt to flee ends with their enduring a longer state of unpleasantness. Buffalo, on the other hand, charge right into the storm when they sense it coming. They don't try to evade the storm and end up minimizing the uncomfortable period.

Refusing to entertain another perspective, refusing to be open-minded on certain issues, stubbornly planting your flag on certain things—this is the way of the cow! Instead of evading the issues or reluctantly engaging the

3. Rory Vaden, *Take the Stairs: 7 Steps to Achieving True Success* (New York: TarcherPerigee, 2012), 33–35.

issues because you have to, charge right in like a buffalo! Here are a few examples of things you can do:

- If you attend a church that uses a modern worship style, visit a more traditionally liturgical church. Read about its traditions and why some Christians prefer that style.
- If you've grown up in the Arminian tradition, choose to write a paper arguing for Calvinism.
- If you have been taught that evolution is the proper scientific interpretation for answering the origin question, choose to research the arguments for intelligent design.
- If you grew up in a denomination that only ordains men for pastoral leadership, choose to write a paper exploring the reasons why some churches come to a different conclusion on this topic.

In short, seek to understand positions that are unfamiliar to you. Through all of these types of "buffalo charges," remember that taking an open and honest look is key. Very often, we read about concepts and different opinions with the intent of finding the holes in their arguments and to re-entrench ourselves in our previously held opinions. This is not an honest look. You don't need to change your opinion, but entering into respectful dialogue in order to better understand issues is the path of wisdom.

COMMIT TO STUDYING BIBLICAL LANGUAGES

One of the particularly uncomfortable parts of your studies will likely be learning Greek and Hebrew. These classes stand on the horizon like looming mountains for most seminary students, creating a range of emotions from uneasiness to flat out fear. There are several reasons that students feel apprehensive about learning Greek and Hebrew. Some may question its usefulness and others may be downright hostile toward the idea. Many are afraid that, given the mammoth task of learning a language, they will not be up to the challenge.

We, and your professors, were once in the same place you find yourself now. We want to give you encouragement for the journey, explain why most seminaries today are still committed to teaching future ministers how to engage with the biblical text in its original language, and give you some advice on how to navigate what for many students is the most difficult part of their seminary studies. By the end of the chapter, we hope you'll agree that Greek and Hebrew are worth the effort.

THE NEED FOR MINISTERS WHO KNOW BIBLICAL LANGUAGES

Most schools require (or strongly urge) students to take Greek and Hebrew as part of their core curriculum for the training of ministers. If you are a student, please don't think that your professors came to this decision lightly. Many of your professors have been pastors, and they know that ministry is not an easy job. It is one of the most stressful careers, and it requires a large skill set so you are prepared for its daily challenges. In the midst of all of the various demands of the pastoral office, you must not forget one thing: You are still a minister of God's Word and are called to proclaim that word faithfully and clearly. Thus, you need to be equipped to engage the Bible in the language in which it was written. So while you may question the usefulness of learning Hebrew and Greek in light of the other demands made of pastors, we ask that you trust the expertise and experiences of those who have gone before you. You need language skills to successfully carry out the calling that God has placed on your life.

As a pastor, you are the main spiritual educator in your congregation. Pop psychology, Christian best sellers, or the latest sermon series that has trickled down from a megachurch will not be the catalyst that drives your congregation toward growth or maturity. It will be a combination of things, one of which is *you* as you model serious study of God's Word, as you actively strive toward a life that conforms to God's will revealed in the Scriptures, and as you genuinely delight in learning more and more about God and his word. The main reason for becoming proficient in biblical languages is that you need to be challenged in your study of God's Word so that you can, in turn, challenge those whom you educate and to whom you minister. This is an important part of "becoming the funnel" that we mentioned above.

While it is true that the pastor needs to know the biblical languages for the sake of communicating the biblical message, biblical languages are *not just* for the teaching pastor. Biblical languages are for all believers who are called to ministry and who want to mature in their study and understanding of the biblical text. When I (Ben) started seminary, I had an undergraduate degree in education. I pursued my master's in religious education, never intending on becoming a senior pastor, so I didn't think I needed biblical languages. This is a false belief, and we want to encourage all who are pursuing biblical and theological education that the languages are for you! More moms, dads, teachers, pastors, lay leaders, doctors, mechanics, and farmers need to be able to teach the Word of God effectively in their home and in the church, and one tool in the toolbox for teaching it is an understanding of the languages in which these words were written.

THE BLESSINGS OF BIBLICAL LANGUAGES

Imagine what it would be like to go from a thirteen-inch black-and-white television to a twenty-seven-inch color television, and then finally sit in a theater with 3-D glasses and watch a movie on the big screen. You may fully understand the story and its characters on the first television, and with the second the images are larger and more vibrant; but in the theater, it is almost overwhelming as colors and images get right up close to you. Most people in the pews who read just the Bible and occasionally the study notes are watching the first television. They get the story, enjoy it, and have come to know God and his saving grace. Those readers who also read some commentaries and dictionary articles are reading, perceiving, and enjoying the Scriptures at a different level, as with the color television. But engaging with the text in its primary language is like being in the 3-D theater. You see things that you have not seen before in stories that you know by heart already, because you are now equipped to engage in deeper research and study of the Bible.

Engaging with God's Word in the original languages will also cause you to slow down and see with greater perception than you ever have before. Christians can often become so familiar with the Bible that when they do read it, they skim. Forcing yourself to engage with the text in its original language requires you to slow down and observe. If ever there was a time to slow down and resist the mentality of instant gratification that prevails in modern society, your time with God and engagement with the word is that time.

However, biblical languages do not take you through a mystical portal to secret learning. Moisés Silva writes about competence in Greek:

It is not the primary purpose of language study to provide the means for reaching astounding exegetical conclusions, although sound linguistic training can at least prevent students from adopting inadmissible interpretations. The true goal of learning New Testament Greek [or Hebrew] is rather to build a much broader base of knowledge and understanding than the student would otherwise have. Occasionally, this knowledge may indeed supply fairly direct answers to exegetical questions. But what matters most is the newly acquired ability to interpret texts responsibly on the basis of comprehensive rather than fragmented (and therefore distorted) information. ...

An effective, reliable biblical exposition need not rely on complex discussions of meanings of Greek words or on the supposed subtleties of the aorist tense, but it certainly should arise out of genuine firsthand familiarity the original text.[4]

Once you begin to understand the biblical languages, you will be equipped to understand at a far higher level the intricacies of interpretation and translation. Every English translation of the Scriptures is an interpretation. The translators have worked diligently to produce as accurate a translation as they can, but as we all know, each translation has differences. Once you know the primary languages, you will be able to understand why these translations differ, and you will be able to read and engage with academic discussions surrounding the biblical text.

---

4. Moisés Silva, introduction to *New Testament Greek for Beginners* by J. Gresham Machen and Dan G. McCartney (Prentice Hall, 2003), 10–11.

A banker named Heinrich Bitzer once stated regarding biblical languages: "The more a theologian detaches himself from the basic Hebrew and Greek text of Holy Scripture, the more he detaches himself from the source of real theology! And real theology is the foundation of a fruitful and blessed ministry."[5] The source of our theology, which is the set of beliefs from which we do ministry, is founded on the text of Scripture. The study of God's Word in its original languages is a high and worthy calling that will inform your theology, nourish your soul, and spur you to good works in the future. Your passion for ministry can only be sustained for a lifetime if it is founded on something that is eternal. Your emotions, the encouragement of others, your ministry "wins"—all of these things are fleeting. Our joy needs to be in the Lord, and our delight needs to be in God and his Word. Learning and using the primary languages for a lifetime of study will help you to find joy in the Lord and place your foundation on God (Ps 1:1–3).

HOW YOU CAN PREPARE FOR LANGUAGE STUDY

Each year that I (Danny) have taught biblical languages, I have received numerous emails from nervous incoming students asking what they can do to prepare for introductory Greek or Hebrew beforehand. Should you be in this position, here are some ways you can prepare.

First, get refreshed on English grammar. Consistently, the students who have the least amount of trouble with learning Greek or Hebrew grammar are students for whom English is a second language. This is because they

---

5. Quoted in John Piper, *Brothers, We Are Not Professionals: A Plea to Pastors for Radical Ministry*, Updated and Expanded Edition (Nashville: B&H, 2013), 98.

had learned how English grammar worked in detail as they learned English, so discussions about verbs, nouns, adjectives, dependent clauses, and so on were somewhat fresh in their minds. But native speakers don't dissect their language as they speak and listen to it; they just do it. A lot of time in your introductory Greek and Hebrew courses will be spent referencing and comparing English grammar, and new students are often learning English grammar *and* learning the new grammar of Greek or Hebrew at the same time.

Second, get an overview of how languages (particularly biblical languages) work in a general sense. Students in grade school don't learn much about how languages work and why they work the way they do. Part of understanding how languages work is learning new terminology like "morphology," "phonology," "dialects," and so on. Luckily, there is a great book for students who are preparing to study Hebrew and Greek titled *How Biblical*

RESOURCES FOR GENERAL GRAMMAR STUDY

To reacquaint yourself with English grammar, we recommend a site like englishgrammar101.com. And if you continue to struggle with the grammar during your course, we also recommend two short companion books that connect Greek and Hebrew grammatical concepts with English grammar:

- Samuel Lamerson, *English Grammar to Ace New Testament Greek* (Grand Rapids: Zondervan, 2004).

- Miles V. Van Pelt, *English Grammar to Ace Biblical Hebrew* (Grand Rapids: Zondervan, 2010).

Languages Work.[6] We recommend picking this book up a month prior to starting your first course and reading it through. This will be a tough task for some students, but it will prepare you for the heavy work that is involved in learning these languages.

Third, get your textbooks early and read the introductory chapters (at least). Because introductory Greek and Hebrew courses cover a lot of material, your professor will hit the ground running. You will have homework in the first week. Often students get hamstrung by not having the book when the class begins. Have it with you that first day, and have at least the introductory chapter read.

Fourth, learn the alphabet and begin pronouncing words. Getting your feet wet prior to the course is a good idea. The scare factor that hits some students in that first class will be behind you if you took the time to learn the alphabet and started pronouncing words on your own.[7] After that, start working on pronouncing simple, common words. For this, we heartily recommend Logos Bible Software's modules for Greek and Hebrew pronunciations.[8] You can also practice reading along with some native readers. Again, Logos has a Greek audio Bible, and you can find readings of the Hebrew Bible online.[9]

---

6. Peter J. Silzer and Thomas John Finley, *How Biblical Languages Work: A Student's Guide to Learning Hebrew and Greek* (Grand Rapids: Kregel, 2004).

7. If you are interested in learning either of the alphabets by song, check out Danny's YouTube channel, where you can find Greek and Hebrew alphabet songs. These videos are linked from his website: www.dannyzacharias.net/singing-grammarian/.

8. Greek: logos.com/product/45485; Hebrew: logos.com/product/5960.

9. aoal.org/hebrew_audiobible.htm

DO NOT BE DISCOURAGED

In addition to taking practical steps of preparation, remember that you are probably in a classroom of students who are in the same boat as you. When we get discouraged we often become very individualistic and think, "No one is suffering as much as me!" You are wrong. There are literally thousands of ministers-in-training across the globe who are engaging in the study of the biblical languages, and many of them feel the same way you do! You have many brothers and sisters in Christ alongside you who are learning Greek or Hebrew. On top of that, countless thousands have already trod this path. Fathers in church history, spiritual giants in the faith, and even most pastors whom you read or listen to have hiked this path before you. While undoubtedly many in the past simply did it because they were forced to, many more did it because they believed it was worth the effort. More specifically, they did it because they believed that diligent study of God's Word meant engaging it in the languages in which it was written.

In addition to remembering that you are not alone, it may also be helpful to remember that it is okay to be a beginner. Although seminary students are adults, learning a language often makes us feel like a kid again. You'll forget things, you'll mispronounce things, and you'll ask questions about things you learned only thirty seconds before you asked. This is normal. Don't feel bad about it. The rest of your classmates are feeling the same way, except for that *one* student (there's always one!) who seems to get it easily. This is the anomaly, not the norm.

Also, the nature of learning a language, especially the grammatical portions, is that you will often feel like you don't really "get" it. You will not feel like you understand chapter 3 of your introductory textbook until you are finishing chapter 5. This is normal, and it is why repetition is so important for learning a language. When I (Danny) introduce this to my students, I often use the (admittedly violent) analogy that it is like treading water in a pool. At the beginning of a new chapter your professor will put his or her foot on top of your head and dunk you down. You will struggle for air and eventually get your nose above the surface of the water for a breath, and then the foot will push you down again—week by week, chapter after chapter. This may seem like an odd way to encourage you, but part of encouraging is helping you to recognize the way things will be and to give you the confidence that you have the ability to understand it. You can make it, even when you feel like you are drowning in vocabulary, grammar, and linguistic nuances.

We live in a culture of instant gratification, but that is not God's way. It certainly will not be your experience when learning Greek or Hebrew. It will require hard work, a lot of time consistently carried out in small chunks, much patience, and a good attitude. If you go through your language courses with resentment, you are in for a bitter few months or years. But if you keep the end in mind and recognize from the start that you can do this, then you will enjoy the journey in spite of the work. The church father Jerome said about learning Hebrew: "I thank the Lord that from this seed of learning sown in bitterness I now cull sweet fruits."[10] If you commit yourself to the task and choose to make use of these tools in

---

10. Jerome, *Letter* 125.12, in *St. Jerome: Letters and Select Works*, ed. Philip Schaff and Henry Wace, trans. W. H. Fremantle, G. Lewis, and W. G. Martley, vol. 6, A Select Library of the Nicene and Post-Nicene Fathers of the Christian Church, Second Series (New York: Christian Literature Company, 1893), 248.

later study, you will be richly rewarded in your study of God's Word.

CONCLUSION

God has designed our bodies in a wonderful way: the more we exercise, the stronger we get. The more we do cardio, the stronger our heart pumps and the longer it will last. Our brains work the same way. They get stronger with more use and exercise. Learning Greek and Hebrew will be difficult, as will your seminary education in general. The Apostle Paul says, "Do your best to present yourself to God as one approved, a worker who has no need to be ashamed, rightly handling the word of truth" (2 Tim 2:15). Yet sometimes when students come to seminary they complain about the amount of homework, they are irritated at having to learn new terms and concepts, they are thrown into a crisis when faced with differing theological opinions, and are annoyed at having to learn biblical languages. Do not strive to bypass the approval process. Getting pulled and pushed by the stretching process is good for you, and it shows God that you mean business when it comes to a lifetime of ministry.

Your professors are there to help you succeed, and that includes wading through the crashing waves of opinion on every subject. They are not usually trying to convince you one way or another; they are showing you the wide amount of scholarship on an issue, the differences of opinion by equally well-meaning Christian scholars, and asking you to enter into the fray to make a decision for yourself. It is okay to be overwhelmed at first by this and the other challenges of seminary. With hard work and a decision to embrace discomfort, you will get through it.

CHAPTER 2

Preparing Your Heart

S everal people have used the analogy of the oxygen mask on a plane to stress the importance of taking care of yourself.[1] When you are on an airplane and they show you how to put on the oxygen mask, you are instructed first to put it on yourself before you help others—otherwise you will be no use to anyone. Jesus says the same thing. In the second great commandment, he says "love your neighbor as yourself" (Matt 22:39). If you don't love yourself, you can't properly love others. This means you need to be deliberate about taking care of yourself spiritually, even in a seminary context.

---

1. One example is blogger and best-selling author Michael Hyatt; see "Where do you put yourself in your list of priorities?" michael-hyatt.com/where-do-you-put-yourself-in-your-list-of-priorities. html.

SPIRITUALITY IS MORE THAN FEELINGS

Most students we come in contact with are excited to learn about Scripture so they may follow God's call on their lives by encouraging the body of Christ. Vocationally this looks different for various students, but the passion is almost always present. Yet for many students, it doesn't take long before seminary starts to take a toll on their spiritual life and excitement level.

One reason is that we often think about spirituality as something that is felt, but seminary rarely cultivates feelings (except for those of exhaustion and fatigue). Instead of feelings, seminary seeks to give substance. We can see this difference between feelings and substance when we tell our children we love them. Sometimes they feel this love and other times they don't, but our love is always there. Every day we go to work in part to show our love for our family by providing for them. There is the *substance* of love in this action, but not always the *feeling* of love. When a three-year-old is hanging on your leg begging you not to go to work, he doesn't feel your love, but the love is still there. While conjugating verbs and memorizing dates in church history don't always feel spiritually uplifting, they do contribute something to our Christian growth. Many students enter into a dry time in their seminary careers because they think their spiritual formation ought to revolve around their feelings; yet in seminary, they find that the typical approach by professors is to encourage their minds.

STUDY ISN'T THE SAME AS DEVOTION

A second reason for the desert experience of seminary is that the hours in the day do not change when you pursue a seminary education. You still have only twenty-four hours. In the past you were able to spend thirty to sixty minutes a day keeping your spiritual life vibrant, growing, and healthy. However, in seminary, a typical day may consist of reading about the Reformation for two hours, reading about the Synoptic problem for another two hours, then spending another hour taking what you read and preparing an assignment for class the next day. Here you have spent five hours on "spiritual" activities; as a result you are tired and your mind needs a break from staring at words on a page.

So when given the opportunity to add devotional time to your studies, it is easy to make the justification, "I just spent five hours on spiritual things. Why spend another hour in Bible study, meditation, and prayer?" This can happen for days and weeks (hopefully not months) until you realize that you are in a spiritual desert. Yet, oddly enough, you are spending more time in study *about* the word and *in* the word than ever before in your life.

This is the story of many seminarians. It is a temptation that we ourselves have fallen into at times. You must guard yourself against this temptation now so that you are ready and able to stand against filling your time with study, telling yourself it is the same as devotion. Instead, prioritize spiritual disciplines as you pursue your call to both *know* and *become*.

DIGGING A WELL

Recently Ben and his wife moved to a house out in the country. Years ago, someone dug a well for the house. If the well digger had quit early, digging a shallow well, the water would have dried up by now. Instead, this well digger dug a well deep enough to water the families that have lived in this house—to give them *life*.

You, too, are in the well-digging business. You are digging a well of spiritual depth. This task is challenging because there is no gauge for how deep you will need to dig this well; however, the well you dig will give water to the ministries God will call you to throughout your life. If you abandon the well-digging process too early, at some point in your career and ministry you will run out of water and will be left with a thirsty flock.

John Piper has said, "Raking is easy, but all you get is leaves; digging is hard, but you might find diamonds."[2] Too often, seminary students are content to remain on the surface academically or in their spiritual investment. You must dig deeply in all aspects of your seminary education, especially in your spiritual life and formation. If you do this, you will find cold, refreshing, life-giving water—not only for yourselves, but for those you will water throughout your ministry.

When Ben was young, his father used the Proverbs to teach his three sons. Much of the proverbial advice consists of the admonition to listen to the wise and add to one's learning. We are not perfect, but listen to our experience and add to your learning! Read through the following pages prayerfully, asking the Lord to show you how to apply these challenges and truths in your life so that your seminary experience can be one of deep growth for your own sake, for your family's sake, and for your current and future ministries' sake!

PRIORITIZE YOUR TIME WITH GOD

It seems hard to imagine that someone studying to go into ministry could have a poor relationship with God, but this is a reality for many seminary students (and too many pastors as well!). Throughout your seminary education,

---

2. John Piper, *God's Passion for His Glory* (Wheaton, IL: Crossway, 1998), 29.

your relationship with God must be your number one priority. This prioritization should carry forward throughout your entire life and ministry. When you make your relationship with God your main priority, the rest of your priorities will properly align.

Too often we recognize the need to be balanced individuals and yet incorrectly define balance. Balance does not mean equal investment in all aspects of life. Instead, biblical balance is proper investment in the right things of life. This means that some of your favorite pastimes and hobbies might not make the cut of what is defined as proper investment. We are not going to tell you where the line is regarding recreational activities, such as city league sports teams, fishing, hunting, yoga classes, video games, or whatever else you do. Instead, we want to help you prioritize the foundation stone that leads to successful balance. In the time left over after the foundation stone of your relationship with God is inserted into its proper spot, *then* you will get to fit secondary priorities, like your family and schoolwork, and tertiary ones, such as your hobbies and interests.

Once you have decided that your relationship with God is the priority, you must decide when to invest time in this relationship through the practice of devotional disciplines. Devotional disciplines are daily practices that maturing believers employ as a means for pursuing godliness, such as spending time in prayer and devotional Bible study.[3] Some people like to have their devotional time with God at night and others have it during the day. If you have a system that works, stick with it. If you do not, or if

---

3. This language of the spiritual disciplines as the *means* to godliness comes from Donald Whitney, *Spiritual Disciplines for the Christian Life* (Colorado Springs: NavPress, 2014), chapter 1.

you have the perfect ideal but you never apply the perfect ideal, then we would suggest you need to prioritize time with the Lord in the morning. There is nothing inherently more spiritual about spending your first moments of the day with the Lord, but as all of us understand— life gets busy. The longer the day goes on, the more disorder it brings and the more exhausted we end up. Again, if you have a system that works, keep it. But if you don't have a system that you *actually* employ on a regular basis, we urge you to start getting up in the morning and giving your first moments to the Lord until you are able to commit to another time. We are afraid, based on experience, that if you just keep doing what you are doing by *planning* to "get around to" a regimented devotional time, you will likely get the same dismal results you have had in the past. Either put action to your plan today, or get up early tomorrow!

Like the time of day, you should also decide on an amount of time to spend on your devotional disciplines. Growing up you may have heard a youth pastor, camp evangelist, or chapel speaker challenging you to spend just five minutes a day in the Word of God. Now that you are in seminary or are being called to seminary, you may still think five minutes a day is sufficient. *It is not!* This view of spirituality is similar to the fitness programs that promise us "eight-minute abs." Five minutes, eight minutes, and even fifteen minutes are not enough for the robust discipleship of a minister of the gospel. Do not settle for this simplistic relationship with God! In 1 Corinthians 13:11 Paul says, "When I was a child, I spoke like a child, I thought like a child, I reasoned like a child. When I became a man, I set aside the things of a child." Eventually Paul gave up his childish ways, and if you are preparing for full-time ministry and haven't yet given up these childish ways, it is time!

If five minutes doesn't work, what does? There is no specific amount of time, but you should become less focused on the amount of time and more on what you are doing during this time for God's glory and for your own pursuit of godliness. Commit to the Lord your heart, your life, your time, and your discipline. Spend your mornings cultivating a love relationship with him. Reflect on his goodness, his grandeur, and his glory! Spend the first-fruits of your days committing your ways to him, meditating on his Word, and praying it back to him.

After years of fumbling through our devotional disciplines, we have learned the importance of purposefully spending time with our Lord. We both find our best is when we give God the mornings. This is challenging with small kids at home, but small and deliberate changes over a long period of time have led to extraordinary results.

HOW TO SPEND TIME IN THE WORD OF GOD

An important aspect of spending time with God is spending devotional time in the Bible. God has given his word as a special revelation to us. Without it, we would not know our sinful predicament and God's solution through the mediation of Christ. The Word, thus, becomes the foundation for spiritual formation. It is through the Word of God that we meet with him and hear him. However, many seminarians have trouble reading the Bible devotionally in the midst of their studies. In this section, we will look at three typical challenges seminarians face when it comes to their relationship to the word. Then we will provide practical suggestions for approaching God's Word devotionally while in seminary.

The first challenge is that we don't take the time and effort to complete the hermeneutical circle.[4] The Bible was not written to us as its first-level recipients. It was written to an ancient people in their circumstances. We must read it in *context* in order to understand the *meaning* the author intended, and then we must find the *significance* of this meaning for our time and place. As you read, do not skip any of these steps. If we stop at the context or the meaning, we fail to see what it means for our lives today—in *this* world. If we jump to the significance, we seek a "nugget for today" at the expense of what the author is saying. It is true that God will give wisdom for today and truth for our moments, but we must approach Scripture to hear what *he* said through his authors, not seeking what we want to hear! This is the difference between *exegesis*, which means that we are drawing out the meaning of the text, and *eisegesis*, which means we are reading our own interpretations *into* the text. The first is right and appropriate, and the second is selfish.

As you approach Scripture by seeking the context, meaning, and *then* the significance, you will begin to learn and see things you never saw before. Your relationship with God will deepen. You will be challenged as previous "folk theologies" you may have been taught are revealed for what they are.[5] In your devotional times, a more accurate and biblical theology may replace some of your sacred cows and preferred beliefs.

Our second challenge is in approaching the Word of God submissively. We do not stand *over* Scripture as its

---

4. For more on this circle, see Walter C. Kaiser Jr. and Moisés Silva, *Introduction to Biblical Hermeneutics: The Search for Meaning* (Grand Rapids: Zondervan, 2007).

5. See Grenz and Olson, *Who Needs Theology?*

authority, but we stand *under* its authority. The Bible makes claims over us and our lives. Some of these claims are uncomfortable, some of them are challenging, and some are downright frightening! However, as students of God's Word and eventually as ministers of the gospel, we must practice reading it and adapting our life to it, rather than asking it to be adapted to our life, will, or beliefs.

Third, when we come to the Word, too often we don't approach it expectantly. God does speak through Scripture, and while this Word was not written to us as the first-level readers, it does have a message for us. In the high priestly prayer of John 17, Jesus prays to the Father saying, "Sanctify them in the truth—your word is truth" (v. 17). The Bible is not a cold document with an esoteric message. Those who have been born again have the indwelling Spirit of God, and he speaks to our hearts through this Word. We should come to it each day to hear a message from our God.

However, the message we receive can come from Deuteronomy as often as it comes from Philippians. We must read the Word, listening to its message, but we must come to the entirety of it and not just our favorite books. When Christ was tempted in the desert, he quoted Deuteronomy. The Law and the Prophets were the Scripture that Paul and Peter submitted themselves to daily. Thus, in our own devotional practice, we too must learn to listen to the whole Bible expectantly!

Here is some practical advice for those of you who are looking for suggestions on how to become a student of the Word—both in mind and heart.

1. Use a Bible reading plan. A reading plan will help you to read what you may not normally turn to. For example, Ben's Bible reading plan currently has him in Deuteronomy, Isaiah, Psalms, and Rev-

elation. Danny's plan is reading through the narrative storyline of the Bible with his oldest son. Left to our own choices, we would not be reading as broadly. If reading the Bible is assigned for a particular course, do this during your personal devotion/study time. This may become your "reading plan" for a season or a semester.

2. In addition to your reading plan, have a study plan. (Note: It may take time and practice to develop both of these. Give yourself grace, but do not forsake the pursuit.)[6] A reading plan gives us the whole counsel of God, while a study plan takes us deeper into the Word. Keeping up with both is a hard discipline, and many of you will need to take baby steps toward this goal before you are able to fully implement it, but it will give life. We recommend that while in seminary you coordinate your study time with whatever book of the Bible is taking up a large portion of your studies or your preaching. If you are taking a class on Exodus, spend your study time there. If you are

---

6. Many new seminarians may read this statement and lose hope: "They want me to read *how much*?!" We do not charge you with following a reading and study plan lightly. It requires time, which seminarians often have little of. However, as you move from student to pastor, minister, or professor you need to hold this before you as a goal. On the other hand, do not feel guilty if you have trouble consistently following this discipline. Longtime seminary professor Howard Hendricks wisely said, "Guilt is a poor motivator. It's very powerful, but it's also poisonous to the learning process. It kills the joy that ought to mark firsthand acquaintance with the Word. Guilt drives more people away from the Scriptures than into them." (Howard G. Hendricks and William D. Hendricks, *Living by the Book: The Art and Science of Reading the Bible,* rev. and updated [Chicago: Moody Press, 2007], 15).

taking a class on the parables, spend your study time there. If you are writing an exegesis paper on a particular passage, choose that passage to read and meditate on during your devotional time while you are working on that assignment.

This is a good way to complete the hermeneutical circle mentioned above. The expectation for exegesis papers is most often on the context and what it meant to the original hearer. Choosing to focus on the same passage for your devotional time will allow you to move to the questions of contemporary relevance and personal significance.

3. If you are leading a Bible study or are preaching, choose a passage you are working on for a class. You've already done a lot of the preparation. Applying that preparation in two different streams is not anti-spiritual, but practical.

4. Redeem "lost" time by getting into the Word. If you have a long commute to school, listen to the Bible via an app or CD. You could also listen to sermons or lectures on the Word from a professor who has made their teaching available.

5. Read through a text and make observations about it. For example, Howard Hendricks required his students to read Acts 1:8 and make 250 observations from this single verse.[7] Ben has adapted this practice and challenges his students to spend time marinating in Romans 8. If you have exhausted this chapter after these 250 observations, then move on. If you can find more, keep at it until you have no more. Then move on to the next chapter. This approach combines the discipline of Bible study,

---

7. See Hendricks and Hendricks, *Living by the Book,* chapter 6.

meditation, and journaling all in one fluid practice. The art of observation is a crucial one and is, sadly, often ignored in our rush to move on to other things.

Much of this advice boils down to the need to practice studying with your head and your heart. Historically, we have separated the two in seminary; we have courses on systematic theology offered by the theology department, and courses on discipleship offered by the pastoral ministries department. While expertise and sub-expertise is a reality of the modern educational system, too often we disallow theologians from talking about discipleship, and we keep practitioners away from teaching the text.

BIBLE READING PLANS

At the time of this writing, Ben is following M'Cheyne's Bible Reading Plan (bibleplan.org/plans/mcheyne), which is a good place to start for those of you who struggle to know what to read. However, it is just one of many that are available, and *any* plan is better than no plan! Here are a few options:

The Bible Project Reading Plan: jointhebibleproject.com/reading-plan

The YouVersion Bible app has a variety of plans: bible.com/reading-plans

Connect the Testaments: A One-Year Daily Devotional with Bible Reading Plan, by John D. Barry and Rebecca Van Noord: lexham-press.com/products/36567

Other plans include the Chronological Reading Plan, Daily Light on the Daily Path, Daily Office Lectionary, and Every Day in the Word Reading Plan. All these can be found through a quick internet search.

We academicians have aided in creating this head/heart dichotomy, and we apologize. Students should be encouraged to approach their theologically oriented classes with their heart fully engaged and approach their leadership classes with their mind equally engaged. The same goes for your reading of the Word—read with your head and your heart! This will cause you to slow down, and that is a good thing.

BE INTENTIONAL IN PRACTICING DISCIPLINES

The goal of Christian spirituality is godliness. While godliness is never completely attained in this life, we can be helped along the way by practicing spiritual disciplines. Much has been written on spiritual disciplines, and we commend to you the wise insight offered through various texts.[8] Our goal here is not so much to describe all the spiritual disciplines as it is to make a few comments on how one might use them during seminary.

Richard Foster introduces his classic *Celebration of Discipline* with his own story of why he started exploring the historic disciplines of Christianity. He started because of his need:

> Fresh out of seminary, I was ready to conquer the world. My first appointment was a small church in a thriving region of Southern California. "Here," I mused, "is my chance to show the denominational leadership, nay, the whole world, what I can do."

---

8. See Foster, *Celebration of Discipline*; Whitney, *Spiritual Disciplines for the Christian Life*; Dallas Willard, *The Spirit of the Disciplines: Understanding How God Changes Lives* (San Francisco: HarperOne, 1988); and Adele Ahlberg Calhoun, *Spiritual Disciplines Handbook: Practices That Transform Us* (Downers Grove, IL: InterVarsity Press, 2015).

Believe me, visions of far more than sugar plums were dancing in my head. I *was* sobered a bit when the former pastor, upon learning of my appointment, put his arm on my shoulder and said, "Well, Foster, it's your turn to be in the desert!" But the "sobering" lasted only for a moment. "This church will become a shining light set on a hill. The people will literally flood in." This I thought, and this I believed.

After three months or so I had given that tiny congregation everything I knew, and then some, and it had done them no good. I had nothing left to give. I was spiritually bankrupt and I knew it. So much for a "shining light on a hill."

My problem was more than having something to say from Sunday to Sunday. My problem was that what I did say had no power to help people. I had no substance, no depth. The people were starving for a word from God, and I had nothing to give them. Nothing.[9]

Don't let this be your story!

Embracing spiritual disciplines during seminary requires intentionality. Just like time with the Lord and time with the Word, the two disciplines we discussed above, other spiritual disciplines require purposeful investment. However, this requires time, and time is a precious commodity in the life of a student. But let us assuage your fears: You do not need to practice each discipline separately for a certain amount of time every day. Richard Foster lists twelve spiritual disciplines in his book; if you were to practice each for thirty minutes a day,

---

9. Richard Foster, *Celebration of Discipline*, xii–xiii.

then a quarter of the day would be gone before you left your house in the morning (or more likely, afternoon). It would be even more difficult to take this approach with Adele Calhoun's list, which includes over forty disciplines. This would take at least twenty hours a day!

LISTS OF SPIRITUAL DISCIPLINES

There is no definitive list of spiritual disciplines because many different practices can be used as a discipline. Here are the lists found in four popular books on spiritual disciplines:

- Richard Foster, *Celebration of Discipline*, lists inward disciplines (meditation, prayer, fasting, study), outward disciplines (simplicity, solitude, submission, service), and corporate disciplines (confession, worship, guidance, celebration).

- Dallas Willard, *Spirit of the Disciplines*, lists disciplines of abstinence (solitude, silence, fasting, frugality, chastity, secrecy, sacrifice) and disciplines of engagement (study, worship, celebration, service, prayer, fellowship, confession, submission).

- Donald Whitney, *Spiritual Disciplines of the Christian Life*, lists Bible intake, prayer, worship, evangelism, serving, stewardship, fasting, silence and solitude, journaling, and learning.

- Adele Calhoun, *Spiritual Disciplines Handbook*, lists sixty-two disciplines under the broad headings of worship, opening oneself to God, relinquishing the false self, sharing one's life with others, hearing God's Word, incarnating the love of Christ, and prayer.

Instead, practice spiritual disciplines in harmony. For instance, as you approach Scripture in the morning, you might approach it prayerfully, meditatively, and with a pen in hand. Here are four disciplines that are practiced together! Likewise, confession, celebration, and worship can all be practiced collectively and harmoniously in small or large group settings.

Seminarians should make it a practice to work all or most of these spiritual disciplines into their lives. There are, however, circumstances that make some of these harder. For those with health issues, fasting from food may not be an option, but you can certainly fast from entertainment, coffee, or something else that your appetite craves. For those with small kids at home, silence and solitude would be a dream, though not likely a reality—this is a big reason why Danny started the habit of waking up early! Recognize that life is cyclical. Many of the challenges that are confronting you now will not be there in ten years, but a different set of challenges will be present. So practice what you can practice now—but push yourself. Don't be content with the status quo! Raise the bar a bit higher than it is comfortable to reach. This will be good for you and your spiritual formation.

Find ways to hold yourself accountable to various disciplines. Seminary is a unique time where men and women gather from around the world to prepare for ministry service. Use this setting to foster your disciplines. Gather with like-minded students to pray about your classes and that the lectures will result in your equipping. Find a classmate with whom you can explore discipleship, not as a curriculum, but as a relational practice commissioned by Christ. Find peers that will hold you accountable to your pursuit of holiness.

In particular, it might be helpful to seek out accountability in fasting or evangelism, two of the disciplines that are often more difficult to cultivate.[10] Regarding fasting, Foster tells us that saying no to the "selfish child" that lives inside us is difficult.[11] Likewise, cultivating the thick skin, eternal perspective, and evangelistic zeal that should define a Christian minister usually pushes us outside of our comfort zone. However, it is likely that at least one of your peers will find these disciplines easier than you do. Find these peers and ask them to teach you how to walk through the disciplines of fasting or evangelism—or hold you accountable to regularly practice these disciplines together in community. Seminary is a time where you can leverage the relationships around you for your growth and theirs. Be creative with how you do this, and make sure to do it on purpose!

It is also important to be intentional about preparing your heart to be teachable and to refrain from grumbling. This is the discipline of gratitude. Seminary can be a time to commiserate and gossip with fellow students going through the same things you are. How simple it is to

---

10. To our knowledge, all of the spiritual formation taxonomies include fasting as a discipline; however, Donald Whitney, *Spiritual Disciplines of the Christian Life,* and Kenneth Boa, *Conformed to His Image: Biblical and Practical Approaches to Spiritual Formation* (Grand Rapids: Zondervan, 2001), are the only two taxonomies that include evangelism as a discipline (or facet, according to Boa).

11. "In many ways the stomach is like a spoiled child, and a spoiled child does not need indulgence, but needs discipline. Martin Luther says '... the flesh was wont to grumble dreadfully.' You must not give in to this 'grumbling.' Ignore the signals, or even tell your 'spoiled child' to calm down" (Foster, *Celebration of Discipline,* 57). See also Martin Luther, as quoted by Arthur Wallis, *God's Chosen Fast* (Fort Washington, PA: Christian Literature Crusade, 1971), 66.

complain about the practicality of classes or assignments, about your professors, and any other thing that is making you uncomfortable and causing you lots of work. Gossip, complaining, and grumbling are toxic to you and those around you. Instead, choose to learn what you can from your assignments, rather than complaining and wondering why you have to do them. Professors with many years of ministry and teaching experience have decided that these classes, these books, these assignments, and these papers are worth your time and will prepare you for a life of ministry. Prepare your heart to be teachable rather than reluctantly doing things, grumbling all the way. Not only will your time in seminary be more rewarding, but you will be protecting your soul too.

In short, while we strongly encourage you to integrate your studies into the fabric of your spiritual and devotional life, you should not assume that your studies and homework are automatically spiritual exercises. The religious leaders in Jesus' day were devout students of the Torah, yet they did not recognize the messiah in their midst. Do not confuse busyness in seminary with a healthy spirituality. The holy disciplines of prayer and meditation cannot be replaced by studying for a test or writing a book review. Be intentional, and don't give up your devotion and prayer life just because you are busy.

PREVENTING A POISONED WELL

To return to our well-digging analogy, cultivating spiritual disciplines and being deliberate about soul care will help you guard against the poisoning of your well. Even if you have dug a deep well, a little bit of poison can ruin your investment. Poison can be cleaned up and sin can be forgiven, but the damage of sin in your life and in your heart will produce fruit that is rotten. Even after confession, contrition, forgiveness, and restoration, you will still find yourself under many of the consequences of your sins.

A year ago, Ben's parents came to his house to help him work in his yard. He and his father spent the day ripping out some large bushes. While pulling out one of these bushes, his father hit his well cover with his oversized truck tires, cracking the concrete. Before a repair man could come and fix the cover, a large chunk of the side fell into the well. The repair man encouraged Ben to cover the hole since squirrels and other creatures might try to enter the well for a cool summer drink and become trapped in his family's drinking water. With a large tarp and a full roll of duct tape, Ben worked to cover the hole until it could be repaired. However, the light, the world, and the bugs (and perhaps a squirrel) had already crawled in, explored, and contaminated their drinking water, which for a season was unable to gife *life*.

Sin is like this. It looks for little chinks in your armor that it can infiltrate. Satan is interested in the long con, and he is willing to cultivate an appetite for as long as it takes for it to become a raging temptation or addiction. He doesn't mind waiting five, ten, or fifteen years for this sin to bear ruinous, rotten fruit. In fact, he might even prefer this so the sins you struggle with in seminary don't seem to be problematic until you are the pastor of a church, professor of a classroom, or leading your family. This way, when this sin brings death, it also brings much collateral damage. So guard yourself and do not let your well be poisoned. Every sin wants to bring death, and all sin destroys relationships—with God, with others, and with self. D. A. Carson tells a hypothetical story of a man who grew up in the church, married a Christian woman, and even did short-term mission work—but ended up leaving his wife and children to take up with a woman he met at work:

> The reasons for such moral failures may be many and confusing. But in some instances, at least, I suspect that there is very little evidence that the young man (or woman, as the case may be) in question ever made a practice of making hard moral decisions that cost him anything. Doubtless his Christian family and home praised him at every step of his sterling pilgrimage. He made the "right" decisions, but they were so scarcely painful or costly, because so many fine people were assuring him how wonderful he was. He did what he wanted to do. But he had not yet been tested by the kind of temptation that drew him to do something that he wanted to do, but which he would resist simply because resisting was the right thing to do. He had not exercised the kind of faith that cheerfully makes self-denying decisions simply because following Christ demands it, simply because it is right.[12]

Here's the key statement in this story: "He had not yet been tested by the kind of temptation that drew him to something that he wanted to do, but *which he would resist simply because resisting was the right thing to do.*" Do you make hard decisions for the sake of discipline? Do you discipline yourself for the sake of godliness? Even Solomon in all his wisdom had this for his spiritual epitaph: "It happened at the time of Solomon's old age that his wives guided his heart after other gods, and his heart was not fully with Yahweh his God as the heart of David his father

---

12. D. A. Carson, *Basics for Believers: An Exposition of Philippians* (Grand Rapids: Baker, 1996), 57.

had been" (1 Kings 11:4). This is one of the more tragic verses in the Bible. A man that started with such wisdom and potential ended up with a heart that was turned away after other gods. His heart was poisoned by the pursuits of wealth, knowledge, power, and sex.[13]

You are beginning your journey as one called to lead. You will not lead like Solomon (and you probably don't have the wisdom of Solomon). Therefore, recognize your "fall-ability" and commit yourself to the Lord each and every day. This is not a one-time decision, but a daily pursuit. It requires a heart inspection on a consistent basis. This requires guarding yourself from the poison that either comes from direct assault or seeps in subtly over time. Men and women of God must assess their hearts and their spiritual lives continuously. Schedule time to hold up the mirror of the Word of God through steadfast commitment to spiritual disciplines, for the sake of seeing your true self and your honest need. Your need is daily—so guard and practice this pursuit each day and throughout all your days!

CONCLUSION

If you are currently in seminary, you likely already recognize the difficulty of continuing to cultivate your spiritual life while there. This war is never won; we struggled with this and still have to fight the battles for our time and our hearts. Instead of navigating the demands of professors who demand paper submissions, we now navigate the increased demands of our fatherly roles and professorial relationships. Instead of professors holding us to sub-

---

13. For a challenging analysis of Solomon and his temptations see Philip Ryken, *King Solomon: The Temptations of Money, Sex, and Power* (Wheaton, IL: Crossway, 2011).

mission deadlines, it is now publishers who do the same. Looking back to our seminary experiences, there were seasons where we did this well and other seasons where we struggled more than succeeded. Endeavoring to persevere is part of the process. Do not capitulate in the times of struggle, but renew your strength!

Too many of us have believed the lie that someday we will have ample time for all we want to do. However, no matter the season, we always only have twenty-four hours in a day. Invest these hours wisely. Spend these hours on the most important things first, and in doing so you will find more freedom in your time and more life from your investment. As we look back with 20/20 hindsight, we realize the time we had in seminary was much easier to balance than the time we have right now. Between us we have seven kids, each a wonderful wife (who deserves an equally wonderful husband), full-time jobs, academic publishing pursuits, and church involvement. Our lives are busier now than ever, but at the same time we also have cultivated devotional habits that are very healthy. It was not until we reached this "even busier" stage that we recognized the truth that is encapsulated in the title of Bill Hybels's book *Too Busy Not to Pray*. We have come to realize what Martin Luther realized—cultivating our devotional life actually empowers us through the rest of our day. He wrote, "It is a good thing to let prayer be the first business of the morning and the last at night. Guard yourself carefully against those false, deluding ideas that tell you, 'Wait a little while. I will pray in an hour; first I must attend to this or that.' Such thoughts get you away from prayer into other affairs that so hold your attention and involve you that nothing comes of prayer for that day."[14] It helps us gain perspective on our daily habits and pursuits, and reorients our lives around God rather than our own schedule.

Your life will *always* be busy; just ask any pastor and they will probably pine for the stress-free days of seminary. But when something is a priority you will make time for it—plain and simple—so make your well-digging a priority. Dig your well deep! Let the depth of the well you dig during this season of your life be deep enough to give water to your soul and your flock for the rest of your life.

---

14. Martin Luther, "A Practical Way to Pray," in Timothy F. Lull and William R. Russell, eds., *Martin Luther's Basic Theological Writings* (Minneapolis, MN: Fortress Press, 2005).

CHAPTER 3

Preparing Your Family

In this chapter, we address the preparation of your family for the seminary venture. First, let us say that we recognize the family looks different in homes across the world. Some students are single parents, some are divorced. Some are seniors returning to school after a successful career in another field. Some have adult children, while others have small children. Some aren't married and would like to be, and some may even feel called to remain single. A few are widowed and plan on living out the rest of their life like the Apostle Paul recommended in 1 Corinthians 7.

While we spend significant time addressing how to prepare spouses for seminary and how to encourage them throughout, we acknowledge that some of you don't have a spouse. We still think this chapter will be valuable. You will know married people in your ministry and go to class with married peers. Some of the information in this chapter is also transferrable to other relationships, such as with your parents, grandparents, your nieces or nephews, or the kids in your youth group whom you are mentoring.

We hope you will read this chapter through the lens of your life, seeking to apply our encouragement in your life context. Throughout this text, whenever we refer to married students or their spouses, please try to find ways to apply our challenges to your life.

IGNORANCE IS NOT BLISS

Seminary will change you. The good news is that if you are in the midst of fulfilling your call from God, then this change is what God has planned for you. But like any change that happens to one person in a relationship, it is bound to have an effect on the relationship and the other person. Sadly, because of the stresses and strains of seminary, there are numerous cases of seminary students who have endured strained marriages, gone through divorce, or broke with their church family—all while in school for the purpose of preparing themselves for ministry. Years ago, Mikala Anne Legako wrote a dissertation exploring the experiences of graduate student spouses titled "Graduate School and Marriage: Life Was Much Happier When We Were Ignorant Christians."[1] For at least some of the subjects of her study, the stress and strain of graduate studies seemed not to be worth the end result of the education.

The truth is that all growth requires some strain. Your muscles strain when they get stronger. Your bones strain when you grow taller, and your mind and your heart will strain as you push yourself to new depths of study. Simi-

---

1. Mikala Anne Legako, "Graduate School and Marriage: Life Was Much Happier When We Were Ignorant Christians" (PhD diss., Rosemead School of Psychology, 1995).

larly, your relationships will also feel strain, but you can minimize this strain by thinking through how you want to move forward in your seminary career and how you are going to lead your family on this journey.

There are three ways to proceed through seminary (and ministry) with a family. The first is to *lead* them on mission, the second is to *drag* them on mission, and the third is to *abandon* them for the mission. Those who choose the first way reap the rewards of a family who walks with them throughout their calling. Those who choose the second or the third way might have some positive effect on the lives of others, but tragically not on the lives of their family. Some of these are able to reconcile with their family along the way, but many will lose their family in the process of following their call. Do not let this be your legacy! Instead, cultivate your relationship with God as the first priority, and cultivate your relationship with your family as your second priority.

MAKE YOUR SPOUSE A PRIORITY

If you are married, or even if you are moving toward marriage (when you are engaged or have a serious boyfriend or girlfriend), your spouse or significant other has to remain a priority while you are in seminary. We challenge you to start thinking through how the changes involved with seminary will impact you and those around you. The better prepared you are for this and the more you communicate these changes, the better prepared all involved will be for this season of study.

Seminary is going to begin to consume your life. If you do not have a supportive spouse, this will prove to be a very difficult time for you—not impossible, but not necessarily pleasant. Thus you need to make sure you don't get tunnel vision, thinking only about *your* degree, *your* pursuits, *your* calling, and *your* formation. You need to lift up your eyes and see that person God has given you as a husband or wife.

All seminary students should remember that their spouses, whether they are working on their own degree or working to support the seminary student, have their own passions and calling. They may or may not get the same opportunity to put life on hold in order to pursue their interests. While the call to seminary is unique and important, it does not outrank their vocation. Don't play the "God card" as an excuse for laziness or to justify your own selfishness.

Similar to this card is the "I've got to study" card. This is a legitimate requirement in seminary, but if you are going to play this card (which you will need to do on a regular basis), make sure you are actually studying like a steward entrusted with the most precious commodity—time. If you are studying at a local restaurant during March Madness, it is likely that church history will not be your priority. If you miss time with your husband or wife, if you miss important moments with your kids as they grow up, or if you miss out on the family discipleship that is required of parents by God (Deut 6), then you are missing out on something vitally important and necessary. Make sure the reasons you are missing are thoroughly defensible—not to us, but to the Lord. As Paul says, we work as if we were serving Christ (Eph 6:5).

HOW SPOUSES GROW THROUGH
THE SEMINARY EXPERIENCE

Ben's dissertation was a study similar to the one mentioned above, but his question differed slightly. In a nutshell he asked, "What are the spiritually formative experiences of seminary spouses?" He was curious how spouses grew as a result of the seminary experience. Not surprisingly, there were experiences that enhanced the spouse's spiritual formation and experiences that detracted from the spouse's spiritual formation. The enhancing experiences revolved around three subthemes. These were *relational* enhancers, *intellectual* enhancers, and *practical* enhancers. Each of the spouses interviewed in this study touched on how seminary positively impacted them in these three realms.

First, seminary spouses shared that they grew in their faith because of their relationship with their student-spouses. As the student grew closer to the Lord, so did the spouse. The spouse grew because of observing the growth in the student. This clearly indicates that digging your well deep will have a positive impact on your spouse's relationship with Christ. In general, the people you surround yourself with have a great impact on your spiritual formation. Your peers in seminary should encourage you to become more committed, devotional, rigorous, and passionate. If you take home this same type of renewed life, you will find a spouse who is similarly encouraged by your commitment, devotion, and rigorous, passionate pursuit of Christ-likeness. During your seminary career, invest in your spouse's formation by living the Christian life in front of them. This requires that you meet with the Lord on a daily basis, spend time reading the Word, practice spiritual disciplines, and commit to the church as well as the mission of the Christian life. Doing all of this in front of your family will indicate to them the importance you place on your discipleship. Over time, it will encourage your spouse's spiritual growth.

However, you should be careful about sharing experiences with your spouse that would be a burden. One of the more difficult things for seminary couples is when the student is exposed to new ideas and ways of thinking about God, the world, the Bible, and so on. You may be confused or frustrated, and you'll go to your partner to try to process things. When this happens, don't forget that your spouse is not with you in class and reading the same material. You are repeating it secondhand when you are just beginning to grasp the subject, and you are emotionally charged about it. Your spouse will often replicate your emotion without the accompanying understanding, and join you in your feelings—but this may also foster critical feelings about that seminary, or that professor, and resentment for "putting you through this." While you may come to a happy resolution through your continued studies, you may never have the chance to reengage in this conversation at home, helping your spouse to reach a similar resolution.

We do not want to dissuade you from talking with your spouse, but do so with wisdom. You will be rapidly expanding your mind into different areas in a way your spouse won't always have the time to keep up with. Be sensitive to that. This will be true in ministry as well; there will be times when you cannot break confidence, or when you should not share discussions because you do not want to sour the opinion of your spouse toward the church or another staff member. You want your spouse to respect the seminary, and in the future you will want your spouse to respect and love the church. Your spouse has not been called to deal with the same things as you, so be wise about how you process things at home.

Many schools allow spouses to attend along with you. If your spouse has the time and interest, this may be a great way to spend time together and be able to discuss the material and readings in particular courses. If your seminary has weekly chapel, as most do, this may be another way for your spouse and even children to feel part of the seminary community.

The second theme in Ben's research revolved around intellectual enhancers. Seminary spouses described how they grew in their faith because the student was in a place where their learning and understanding matured. This happened in numerous ways. Many of the students would bring home ideas and share them with their spouse. As mentioned, these ideas can encourage or discourage, so be careful in how you bring home these ideas and new insights. One wife, who happened to be the spouse of an online student, explained that because her husband worked full time and had to take classes in the evening, he didn't have peers surrounding him with whom he could process his course reflections. She got to be that peer. In his growth, she explained that she became more adept in theology and was better prepared to articulate her own beliefs. Another described how the books the student brought home shaped her own formation. Most of the spouses interviewed also identified how the practice of proofreading the student's papers had a formative impact on their own ability to understand their faith. One spouse said, "I am not going to read a 200-page book, but I can read a twelve-page book review." As a student, what you bring home does cross over into your family. Practice bringing home wisdom and keen insights into your faith, and do so with intention.

Third, spouses in this study found that the seminary experience enhanced their faith practically. It seemed that seminary opened the eyes of these spouses to the fact that they had a role to play in the body of Christ. Going into seminary, many of them thought ministry was for the one training to be a "professional," but they soon realized this was not the case. Many of the spouses talked about discipleship, church planting, and the great commission and their own role in these practical outworkings of faith.

If this practicality is something that would encourage a spouse's personal growth, you (the student) should be active in cultivating this realization in your spouse. In many seminaries, a ministry practicum is required for students. You may want to bring your family along for this when it is wise and they are able. However, as above, we also have a word of caution here. Remember that while you are in seminary, and especially after seminary, *you* are the one called to professional ministry—not them. Ministry spouses are quite often involved in ministry, but it is their own choice to use the gifts God has given them. In some churches, getting "two for the price of one" is often wrongly assumed. You need to be the one to speak up about this and make it clear that you are the one called to ministry and ministry training in seminary, not you + your spouse.

MAKE YOUR KIDS A PRIORITY

"Children are a gift from the LORD" (Psalm 127:3 NLT). This is absolutely true, but it is equally true that they can be sanctifyingly *exhausting*. A mentor of Ben likes to say, "If parenting isn't the most exhausting job you've ever had, then you are doing it wrong." We love our children, but parenting is hard work. The challenges of parenting are intensified if you are trying to work while pursuing a master's degree and maintaining some semblance of a relationship with your spouse. However, as busy as you are and as challenging as this life is, it is your calling. If you ever think that this is something you cannot handle, then it is probably the schooling that needs to suffer or be dropped, never the family! Psychologist and author John Townsend once told a story about going through his doctoral work. He was a single student pursuing the degree with everything he had and feeling as if he were just getting by. One day while talking to a peer who was married with four kids, he asked, "How do you do it? I am barely surviving and I don't have the obligations you have." His colleague replied, "It's easy—I get C's."

We don't want you to set your sights on becoming a C student if you can do better than that. However, we and most seminary professors would rather you get a C in class than get a C in parenthood. Many people have had great ministries with a 2.0 GPA. (However, if you want to get into a doctoral program you will need to adopt a plan for getting good grades that doesn't involve ignoring your family.) Being just an average disciple maker of your children is worse than being an average student. You are one of two divinely mandated individuals on this earth called to be a special and unique discipler of your kids. When you are in ministry later, you will always be able to go back and look up the definition of *antinomianism* should you need it. You cannot go back to when your daughter was five and she was excitedly recounting her realization that in heaven we get to meet Jesus! If you miss the one-time experiences you get while raising your kids, you are missing out. No one can fill in the void you leave when you are not at home or engaged in the lives and discipleship of your children. You need to disciple them on purpose even while you are in school.

While no study that we know of has been done on the spiritually formative experiences of seminary children, we would bet that the processes are much the same as Ben's study above on seminary spouses. Relationships, information and new ideas, and practicing their faith will all enhance your children's growth. Many of the ideas for practicing with your spouse can be adapted to apply to your children, depending on their ages. The key component for discipling them (while in school or out of school) is the level of your intentionality. If you make this your goal and build it into your day and your conversations, it will happen. This is how all plants are cultivated and how all lives mature—slowly and over time.

TIPS FOR STAYING CONNECTED TO YOUR FAMILY

1. For those still considering seminary, ask your spouse if they have any concerns related to your plans for enrollment. Listen to your spouse's feedback, which requires considering and internalizing what they say. For instance, perhaps your spouse challenges you with the observation that you are not generally good at finishing projects, suggesting that it may be unwise to commit the money and time since you might have trouble finishing a course or a degree. This is good, valid, and necessary feedback that you will need to work through together in the planning process.

2. Another practice we find valuable for those who are considering seminary, but are still processing whether they want to commit, is to *fully* explain to your spouse why you want to enroll in seminary and why you think God is calling you to further your education. This will help you process the decision for yourself, and also help your spouse to get on board.

3. While in seminary, be sure to keep a regular date night or continue doing other things you regularly do together. This might not happen as often, but it can't disappear either. Holding on to that time where school and ministry does not have your

attention is a significant way for you to indicate that your family is still a priority to you.

4. Depending on the personality of your spouse, you may want to challenge them to read either one book a semester from your courses or one book per course. Choose a book you know that will be readable, encouraging, and edifying. In an introductory course Ben teaches, he has used Kelly Kapic's text *A Little Book for New Theologians*. This would be a fantastic book for a seminary spouse to read. It is short, digestible, and one that can facilitate intellectual and relational dialogue between you.[2]

5. Ben requires his new seminary students to conduct a SWOT analysis of themselves with the assistance of their spouses (or children, or a close friend or relative). In Ben's classes, many of the spouses identify procrastination in studies as a weakness. If your spouse identifies this, recognize that you need to make some changes in your life and in the budgeting of your time (which we hope to help you with in later chapters). Your opportunities and threats are often harder to identify. However, typically an opportunity comes from investing in and

---

2. Other books we have used in our classes that would be readily assimilated without the seminary technicalities are D. A. Carson, *Praying with Paul* (Grand Rapids: Baker, 2014); Sam Storms, *Signs of the Spirit* (Wheaton, IL: Crossway, 2007); Stephen Nichols, *Bonhoeffer on the Christian Life* (Wheaton, IL: Crossway, 2013); Harold Myra and Marshall Shelley, *The Leadership Secrets of Billy Graham* (Grand Rapids: Zondervan, 2005); Stanley J. Grenz, David Guretzki, and Cherith Fee Nordling, *Pocket Dictionary of Theological Terms* (Downers Grove, IL: InterVarsity Press, 1999).

honing your strengths. Likewise, a threat comes from not harnessing or limiting your weaknesses.

6. Another practice is to ask your spouse to proofread your papers for clarity and/or technicality (depending on their strengths). This helps your spouse to see the fruit of your hard work and is valuable for you as much as it is for them. It also gives the two of you something to discuss and encourages your spouse to learn something about their faith along the way.

7. Include your spouse (or your children) in your practicum assignments where you can, particularly those that require you to share the gospel with a neighbor or a stranger. Let them see you articulating your faith, stumbling for the right words, and praying with those who are hurting. All of this contributes to their formation and encourages them to

SWOT ANALYSIS

A SWOT analysis is a reflection tool designed to explore an individual's **S**trengths, **W**eaknesses, **O**pportunities, and **T**hreats. This assignment opens up dialogue between spouses. This is a no-holds-barred conversation on what the spouse sees in the life of the student.

To do this, set aside at least one hour to sit down with your spouse and ask them about your strengths, weaknesses, opportunities, and threats. Commit to listening and not getting defensive. Start with a pen and paper in hand, and write down what you hear and think—but make sure to listen! We all have strengths and we all have weaknesses, so don't get bitter when your spouse is able to identify weaknesses.

see once again that this is not just something you are studying, but something that is turning you into the man or woman that God is calling you to be![3]

8. Budget your time. You can keep things from piling up on you at the last minute by planning out each week, comparing your school calendar and your family's calendar. Just like budgeting your money is painful at first, budgeting your time and your focus is also painful. However, it is beneficial and it needs to be done. Just like with your money, if you don't plan where your time goes, you will be left wondering where it went.

9. Set boundaries for your schoolwork time, and focus on it during that time. When you are studying, focus on studying (do not catch up on your fantasy football team). Even today, when we need to get something done in a timely manner, we don't do it from home. When you have young children, an hour away is worth three hours of semi-focused/semi-distracted work from home. We would prefer to take the hour away and then return with the mindset that we are home now to focus on our family. It is too difficult for children to understand why you won't play with them when you just seem to be sitting at a desk.

10. Likewise, set boundaries by delineating no-homework periods of the day. Let your family know, for instance, that from the time you get home until their bedtime, you are not allowed to do homework unless it has been agreed upon beforehand (exam

---

3. An excellent book from the perspective of a child learning about ministry from watching a parent is D. A. Carson's *Memoirs of an Ordinary Pastor* (Wheaton, IL: Crossway, 2008).

time, for example). Be active in interacting with your family during this time. When you're home, *be present*. We live in an age of extreme distraction, particularly with smart phones. Both of us love technology and have the latest phone and tablet, but even if we have all of the notifications turned off, we still struggle with the technological distractions. It is still difficult to get out of "work mode," and we both are reminded frequently of our need to focus on our families when we have committed to a work-free evening. Our hyper-connected world has made it especially hard to be present, and if you are a parent, it is often your kids and your spouse that suffer the most when you are not present. Set boundaries, and enlist those most important people to help you enforce them when you falter. Your family deserves your full attention, and God has designated your first and most important ministry to be to your family. Your procrastination and distraction has real consequences beyond the seminary walls.

11. Ask your spouse to read appendix 3, "A Word to Spouses," at the end of this book, and then come together to talk through their reactions.

CONCLUSION

In Ben's research, the biggest complaint of spouses regarding seminary was the amount of time it required of the student and how often this pulled them away from family interaction and responsibility. If you are a spouse or a parent, your responsibilities do not cease just because you become a student. You will have to work with your wife or husband to decide whether your responsibilities at home can change. Be clear on your priorities and responsibilities and adjust your life accordingly. Be efficient because others are counting on you. You can't expect your spouse to carry the load on the home front if you are not making every effort to be as efficient and hardworking as possible. Lounging around in the student cafe because "that's what students do" is a dressed up way of stealing time from more important people in your life. Putting off all your major assignments until the end of the semester and then stressing out will set a tone in your home as well.

You have a high and holy calling to take God's Word and share it with his church and the world, but if you neglect your family, you have killed one of your best avenues for fulfilling this call. If you forsake your family in pursuit of your degree, then you are not practicing your missional mandate to make disciples in the most important context God has given you. Challenge yourself, with the help of the Holy Spirit and accountability partners (including your spouse), to engage in the discipleship of your family throughout your time in school and for the rest of your life and ministry.

PART 2

MANAGING TIME
AND ENERGY

CHAPTER 4

Taking Responsibility

You alone are responsible for your successes and failures in life. While there may be many people at the seminary who are helpful and will guide you through the process, ultimately no one is as invested in your education as you should be. This means you need to accept responsibility and take charge.

Some students rely on the registrar or faculty advisor to make decisions for them and to keep track of their progress through the degree program. Other students do not put in the effort to understand their assignments and end up blaming their professors when a poor mark is received. In both of these cases, students are outsourcing the responsibility for their education to other people. This is a recipe for frustration for the student, professors, and administrators who seek to guide the student in the process. Your time in seminary will go much more smoothly if you make the decision early on to accept responsibility for your studies. This chapter will introduce you to a number of ways you can do just that.

THIS IS YOUR JOB

The first step to taking responsibility is recognizing that if you are studying full time at a seminary, *it is your job*. Treat it that way. Don't sleep in just because your class starts in the afternoon that day. Get up early every day and get to it! If you are not in class, you should be doing work at home or in the library. If you set aside time to work on your own, you'll start to notice that your evenings will be free much more often. You will also find that while your fellow students are cramming, pulling all-nighters, or begging for extensions, you'll be under far less stress because you managed your life well through the whole semester.

Not only is it responsible to treat your studies like your full-time job, but it is also a necessity if you hope to have any semblance of life outside of study. Life quite often looks different for seminary students than it did in college. Seminary students may be working or ministering part time, they may be married and with a family, and they are also getting older. This last point hit home for me (Danny) in the second year of seminary, in which I pulled a (final!) all-nighter in order to meet a publishing deadline for work I was assisting with. I had pulled all-nighters during my undergrad a number of times, but this time was different. The youthful vitality that enabled me to stay up all night in the past had disappeared.

Treating your studies as your full-time job will also help to alleviate stress at the end of a semester. Graduate level study is more demanding than undergraduate level study. Add to this the different life circumstances seminary students are in, and the end-of-semester stress may be a recipe for disaster, both mentally and emotionally. I (Danny) recall several semesters during my graduate studies when I was completely done with my coursework (minus exams) while my peers were just starting their major assignments. It was a *great* feeling. But it was not an accident or luck: I treated my studies like a job. When I wasn't in class, I was in a study room working. Like any student, there were coffee breaks with friends or ping-pong matches, but these were not three-hour tournaments that consumed a whole morning; they were fifteen-to-twenty-minute breaks or lunch hours. Treating your studies like your job, which includes planning your semester (see the next chapter), will help to alleviate the end-of-semester stress to which many students continue to subject themselves.

KEEP TRACK OF YOUR PROGRESS

The program sheet, or degree completion plan, is like a map charting the course of your seminary experience. This sheet, which shows the requirements for your degree, should be available to you at all times. As you move from semester to semester, you will need to decide what classes you can take to fill elective slots, and you will need to ensure that you are taking required courses when they are offered. You should always know where you are in your journey and where you are heading. Keeping and evaluating your program sheet will help you to be prepared for course registration rather than being clueless and having a registrar hold your hand through the process. Knowing your program sheet is doubly important if you are doing dual degrees or planning on a second graduate degree at the same school. In these cases, students may need to take classes in the same semester that will be fulfilling different degrees.

While it is thankfully rare, there have been times where the registrar has to inform students who are expecting to graduate that they are one course short. This scenario is frustrating, but it can easily be avoided if you take responsibility and chart your course through your degree program.

UNDERSTAND WHAT IS EXPECTED

On the individual course level, a syllabus is a contract between you and your professors. They are obligated to stick to the contract and need permission if they are going to make a radical change. This means that you need to accept responsibility for doing the assignments as specified, for holding the professor to the syllabus they have provided, and for seeking immediate clarity for any problems or gray areas within the syllabus.

You also need to understand how much work is involved in your course. A good rule of thumb is that at the graduate level, you should expect to put in *three hours of work for every one hour in class.* Some courses will be more, some will be a little less. If you don't know if it is a "heavy" course, simply ask a student who has been there for a year—the reputation of workhorse professors spreads quickly! Knowing this ahead of time can help you plan your semesters better.

The syllabus is not the only place you have the opportunity to learn what is expected. Unless you have come into seminary with some paper-writing experience, your first few writing assignments will be daunting and feel torturous. But these are learning experiences—a chance to improve.

Whenever you receive an assignment back that isn't an "A," go through the notes and markings your teacher has made. If you do not feel the notations were adequate, or if they were confusing, then book a short appointment with your professor (or the teaching assistant who graded the assignment). Bring the assignment with you and say, "I really appreciate you taking the time to meet with me. Could you please take a few minutes and tell me exactly what I could have done to get a better mark on this assignment?" Then listen, take notes, and ask for clarification. Get feedback so that every mistake becomes a learning experience.

Once you get your assignments back, work through all of the feedback and seek the help of a writing tutor if need be. Mistakes turn into failures only if you do not learn anything from them. They can be your best teachers if you let them.

DON'T WAIT FOR YOUR PROFESSOR

Your syllabus should detail your assignments clearly, or the professor may indicate that specifics on assignments will be forthcoming. If this is the case, be sure that those specifics are discussed as soon as possible. If an assignment is vague and you do not press (and even annoy) your

SEEK OUT ADDITIONAL FEEDBACK

For your first few papers, we would recommend asking up front for more critical feedback. Put a note on the front of the paper (or on the first page of the electronic version) that says something like:

> "Dear Dr. _____, I would very much appreciate it if you would offer me some critical feedback on the assignment. Please do not hold anything back, as I want to learn from my mistakes. Thanks in advance for this extra effort."

professor to give more clarity, then the grade you receive is entirely on you. The professor may have been unhelpful, but you are the one who plunged forward without clarity.

Quickly you will find out the personality of your professors. Some professors are more exact than others, so their assignments are detailed and specific. Whether this is your disposition or not, recognize that it is their disposition and you should work toward following the letter of their law. Other professors tend to give generic ideas for their assignments in hopes that the creativity of the student will come forth in their understanding of the assignment. If you are a detailed student, this will likely annoy you. Spend time trying to, as the saying goes, "nail Jell-O to the wall." The more you ask, the more specific they will become and you will have a better idea of what they are looking for.

Your professors are busy. If you want to have a meeting with them, you need to take the initiative. This is doubly true if you are taking a directed study course or if you are a thesis student. Your professors have many students, are teaching numerous courses, are involved in their own research, and have administrative responsibilities. They are not in charge of your success—you are. So take charge and arrange meetings instead of waiting on your professors. And if you are waiting on your professors to finish something they have committed to do for you, don't be afraid to email or call them about it until it gets done.

KNOW YOUR RIGHTS AND OBLIGATIONS

It may not be a real page-turner, but most seminaries have a student handbook that is written for you. The handbook will detail your rights as a student and any procedures you need to follow if complications should arise. The handbook will also specify what you need to do if you need an extension in a course, extension for your degree, or if you are having a problem with a professor's conduct (missed meetings, not meeting obligations, harassment, etc.).

Another important item that you need to bear in mind is the course drop date. Find out when the last day is to drop courses without academic penalty and mark it in your calendar in bold letters. "Drop" is not a dirty word. In fact, in some circumstances it is the wisest decision you can make. Major personal problems, family tragedies, or even just feeling overloaded are all good reasons to drop a course.

You should also know that you are well within your rights to talk about any academic concerns with your academic dean. Here are some reasons you may want to have a conversation with your dean:

1. **After** discussing assignments with your professor, you (and your classmates) feel that your professor is being unreasonable in their marking.
2. **After** discussing it with your professor, he or she is still changing assignments or dates in your syllabus without class discussion and agreement.
3. **After** discussing it with your professor, you and your peers feel that the workload for the course is far in excess of what is reasonable (remember, grad studies assumes about three hours of work for every hour in class).

My (Danny's) personal tendency is to avoid conflict, so I understand that these discussions can be difficult and awkward. But one awkward conversation can often end up being beneficial for you and your fellow students. During my seminary degree program, I had to challenge the workload of a syllabus with the academic dean—and the dean was the professor for the course! But in the end, he agreed and the workload was reduced. Another time I challenged what I felt was unreasonable grading. This was an uncomfortable discussion, but in the end the professor agreed and changed his grade. (Both of these men ended up being my colleagues a few years later!)

In both of these instances, the conversation was held with the professor directly face to face, not by email and not by going to someone else in the administration. If you have a problem with something your professor is doing, the respectful thing is to have a private conversation. Most of the time, they will appreciate your courage and straightforwardness. It is also very easy to misinterpret the tone of people through email, and quite often people will say something in email (or on social media) that they would never say directly to a person. The last thing you want is a tension-filled email exchange with a professor that could have been easily replaced with a face-to-face conversation.

During these exchanges, be certain that you are clear in your communication. One time as a professor, I was walking through the hallway when a student asked me a quick question regarding a course. I gave a quick answer that I thought satisfied his question, and I continued on my way. It turns out that it wasn't enough, and it deserved a longer discussion. But I did not find this out from another conversation with the student. Instead, I found out from my dean at the end of the semester. What could have been resolved by a follow-up meeting and conversation became a major issue involving multiple parties. All of that confusion and anger happened because we didn't communicate.

On a related note, in cases when you are requesting exemptions from courses, transfers, or substitutions for courses, be sure to follow the correct procedures and talk to the correct people. For instance, your professor or your course advisor cannot typically grant you course exemptions or substitutions. For any decisions made regarding these special requests, ask that the decisions be sent to you by email so that you have official confirmation on any decisions that affect the completion of your degree. In situations like these, your seminary may not always keep all the paperwork you need, so take responsibility for obtaining and filing your own copies. As always, you alone are responsible for your success.

CONCLUSION

When I (Ben) was a young boy, my father taught me the lesson of taking responsibility. He was not interested in having "good kids"; instead he was interested in raising good men (he had three sons). For instance, whenever we would make a mistake, our excuse was, "We didn't mean to!" My dad's response was, "Did you mean *not* to?" This and other fatherly sayings were annoying at the time, but the lessons they were meant to teach assisted in the forming of men from boys. Eventually we learned to take precautions so we would not make mistakes that led to poor consequences.

Likewise, we want to help you recognize that you are meant to mature. Just as Paul said that he put away childish things in his past, we want you to put away poor habits and childish practices that have hurt your maturation. In place of these, cultivate habits of taking responsibility so that your efforts will create great dividends as you invest in this seminary experience.

You are not alone in seminary and you will likely find great help and assistance from your faculty advisor, the dean, or the registrar. However, none of these people are as invested as you should be in the completion of your degree. Get focused, organized, and stay on top of things.

You are an adult, and no one wants to or needs to hold your hand through this process. Take charge and chart your course. Lean on the Lord and those willing to assist, but make sure that you take responsibility.

CHAPTER 5

Managing Your Time

G od has given us all a set amount of hours in the day, and we are each responsible for stewarding that time and for spending it on the priorities he has placed in our lives. Unfortunately, we live in an idle culture. Massive entertainment industries exist solely to help us fill in our idle time, and during times of work, social media often can draw us back into unproductive surfing. We need strategies and tools to help us fight against the cultural current of idleness.

While the topic of productivity sells a lot of books, it is also thoroughly biblical. Not only do we have the example of God himself working for six days at creation (Gen 1), but we have examples in toiling in work (Prov 6:6–11). We see in the parables Jesus' praise for resourcefulness when it comes to investing (Matt 25:14–30) and prudence (Luke 16:1–13). The Apostle Paul also rebukes idleness and praises diligence (Eph 6:5–9; 1 Thess 4:11–12; 2 Thess 3:6–12).

If you want to not only survive but thrive in seminary, you need a plan. We've both been students for the majority of our lives, and both of us learned time and life management on the fly as we were going through our studies. However, eventually we got into a groove. No longer did we have to pull all-nighters or work frantically into the weekend. We want to give you the advice we wish we'd received during seminary.

The key is making a plan at the beginning (of a term, a year, a project, or a class) and sticking to it. This chapter will help you to plan out your semester in the first week, and will also give you some general strategies for making the most of your time so you can set yourself up for success.

MAKE A MASTER PLAN UP FRONT

Once you receive your syllabi for the classes you're taking, you need to process them into your master plan of action. This will *overwhelm* you, but it is better to feel overwhelmed at the beginning rather than the end. Trust us! Find all of the due dates on each syllabus and circle them. For each assignment or test, label them under three headings (you can use different colors of highlighters, for instance): major assignments, minor assignments, and reading.

- A *major assignment* is any project that has a lot of the grade for the course associated with it. Written assignments, tests, exams, papers, and presentations usually fall under this category.
- A *minor assignment* is a project with a small amount of the grade associated with it. These won't take you more than a few hours, at most a day, to complete.
- The *reading* label is for any required reading for your classes.

Keep in mind that the due date of a major assignment, particularly papers, does not dictate when to begin the assignment. Your syllabus does not say, "Start this assignment that is worth 50 percent of your grade two days before the due date." Knowing the due dates gives you the terminal point that you cannot exceed. The step of placing them into your master plan will determine when you will begin working on them, and when you aim to complete them.

If one of the major assignments for a class is a presentation for which you can choose the date, grab one of the earliest available slots. If you can avoid it, don't sign up to do a presentation in the last week of the semester when everything else is due. This will provide positive pressure to propel you into action in the very first week of your studies.

You also need to make sure you are doing things correctly early on. If your syllabus is fuzzy on what exactly a teacher is looking for, get clarification right away. Also ask around and find out about your teacher's marking style. If your teacher moonlights as a member of the grammar police, then put extra time into that. If your professor expects very specific types of footnotes, then invest time into that. Don't be afraid to ask your professor for example papers or other forms of guidance. Some professors are very good at providing documents to help you understand what is expected, while other professors can leave you feeling a little lost. As much as you are able, seek clarity on your assignments, because in the end you alone are responsible for your assignment (see the previous chapter). No matter how productive you are, if you are headed in the wrong direction you are wasting your time! Know exactly where you are heading before investing your time and energy.

It is also important to determine from your syllabus how much weight is put on class participation. If it is significant, then you need to break past any possible shyness and find ways to engage in class. I (Danny) tended to be a student who did not say much, especially in larger classes. One class in particular forced me to pay attention to the class participation mark, as the professor was actually keeping mental tally of each student's participation in class. A third of the way through the semester, the professor asked me why I never said anything and told me that my participation mark is going to suffer. Prior to this, I had thought that the participation mark was just about showing up to class. For some professors this may be the case, but for most professors they want to see that you are mentally engaged.

As professors, we are also aware of how distracted students can be in class with social media. When we see students checking their phones in class, or staring at their laptop without ever looking up at the professor, these are almost always signs of a disengaged or distracted learner. Students that are perpetually like this will lose participation marks, so don't be one of those students.

ARRANGE YOUR CALENDAR

Now that you have created your master plan, get your assignments into a calendar system and put into your calendar other events that you are committed to, like family, work, and ministry obligations (see chapter 10 for calendar app suggestions). You need to lay out what you'll be doing every single week of your semester and stick to it. Every week you should be working on items under the three labels: you will have a weekly reading schedule, small assignments to finish, and major assignments to work on. For a typical schedule you will be working on between one and four minor assignments each week, and one or two major assignments each week. It may be that a particular minor project goes by a lot quicker than the time you have allotted. This will give your schedule some flexibility for those times when minor projects take a little more time than you thought, and will also provide more time for working on your major projects.

By the end of your first week of class you should begin working on a major project, even if it is not due until the last day of class. So every day on your calendar there should be no wondering what to do—do your reading, then do your minor assignment(s), then do your major assignment(s). We recommend working in this order so that you have some positive stress in your calendar—you should always be pushing to get the reading and minor assignments done so that you can get to the major assignments, because the largest chunks of your marks are tied to them. And keep an eye on your master plan. Review it daily and weekly. A close due date always takes priority over everything else.

The final piece of the calendaring process is determining your study blocks, as this is where all of the assignments will actually get done. As much as you are able, commit yourself to a weekly routine that includes set-in-stone study blocks. Treating studies as your full-time job means not only committing yourself to being in class, but committing yourself to putting the time in outside of class. This is often difficult to commit to because no one (but yourself) is expecting you. Your attendance is expected at class and you are expected to show up for your job or ministry position, but it is often only you who is holding yourself accountable to your study blocks. This is why you must be ruthless with yourself and be your own taskmaster.

TROUBLESHOOT AND ADJUST

If you work this plan and find that you cannot keep up, or too many of your assignments are being pushed forward to the next week, several things might be happening:

1. You may be taking too much time on your reading and small assignments. Remember to read actively (see chapter 9) and don't distract yourself with time wasters. When you are doing your reading and small assignments, let your looming major assignments exert some pressure on you.
2. You may be afraid of "closing the deal." If you have worked hard on a major or minor assignment, completed it early as suggested, and done another round of editing (by yourself and perhaps someone else), then hit the print or send button and check that item off your list!
3. You may not actually be putting in the quality or quantity of time that is necessary. Are you working hard and being productive and efficient, or are you working for fifteen minutes, then checking Facebook, then reading for five minutes, then chatting for ten minutes, then texting someone, then working for fifteen minutes, and so on? For advice on productivity, including how to effectively work during your homework blocks, see the section "Choose to Turn off Distractors" below.

If you are honestly putting in the time, working efficiently and not procrastinating, and are still not able to keep up, then you need to start thinking seriously about dropping something. It may be one less work shift, scaling back your ministry commitments, or dropping a class. One benefit of establishing your master plan early is that it will help you recognize if you need to scale back before it is too late—in particular dropping a class without academic penalty.

Particularly if you have a part-time job or ministry position, you will need to adjust your schedule on a weekly basis. But the beauty of blocking time for homework is that those blocks can move around to fit and adjust to your schedule. Following this plan and treating your studies like your full-time job will also make unexpected events less stressful for you, because if you follow this plan, you will often be one to three weeks ahead of schedule. Take control of your time, be ruthless about your schedule, and you will be able to stay on top of your homework.

Example Week Schedule

	Sat	Sun	Mon	Tue	Wed	Thu	Fri
Morning	optional study	Church	Class 1	Study	Study	Class 4 • reading due	Study
Afternoon	optional study		Study	Class 2 • reading due	Class 3 • item due	Class 5	Study
Evening	P/T Job	optional study	P/T Job	Study	Study		P/T Job

Study Time

READING
- [ ] Class 2 text ch.5 (due Tue)
- [ ] Class 4 ch.3 (due Thur)
- [ ] Class 3 ch.4 (due next Thur)
- [ ] Class 5 ch.3 (due next Mon)

MINOR
- [ ] Class 3 reflection assign. (due Wed)
- [ ] Class 5 quiz (due next week)

MAJOR
- [ ] Class 2 book review (due next week)
- [ ] Class 1 paper (due in 3 weeks)

BATCH YOUR TASKS

Once you have your master plan in place, you have put it in your calendar, and you have committed to adjusting it as necessary, you still need to manage your time on a day-to-day basis. One helpful way to do this is by batching your tasks. If you have ever worked at a fast-food franchise, you know that there are assembly line systems for building the meals. At a burger restaurant, one person assembles the burger, one person cooks the fries, another person gets the drink. Each of these have separate stations with their own space. This batching of similar tasks is how they can handle high volumes of orders.

As much as you are able, you should consider ways that you can also batch your seminary tasks. For instance, I (Danny) try as much as possible to only check my email twice a day when I am in the office. And when I do this, I have devoted that time to acting appropriately on those emails so that I can remove them from my inbox. Once I am done going through my inbox, I close my email application and move on to the next task.

Another example is library work. Depending on your campus and location, a trip to the library may take up a

RECOMMENDED BOOKS ON PRODUCTIVITY

Loehr, Jim, and Tony Schwartz. *The Power of Full Engagement: Managing Energy, Not Time, Is the Key to High Performance and Personal Renewal.* New York: Free Press, 2004.

Maxwell, John C. *Make Today Count: The Secret of Your Success Is Determined by Your Daily Agenda.* 1st Center Street ed. New York: Center Street, 2008.

McKeown, Greg. *Essentialism: The Disciplined Pursuit of Less.* New York: Crown Business, 2014.

Newport, Cal. *Deep Work: Rules for Focused Success in a Distracted World.* New York: Grand Central Publishing, 2016.

Rubin, Gretchen. *Better Than Before: Mastering the Habits of Our Everyday Lives.* New York: Crown, 2015.

Vaden, Rory. *Procrastinate on Purpose: 5 Permissions to Multiply Your Time.* New York: Perigee, 2015.

significant chunk of your day. If you have several assignments that require library work, try and do the library work for all of the assignments at the same time.

A final example is small assignments associated with reading. If you are required to do any sort of small assignment with an assigned reading (such as a short book report), do it immediately after you read so that it is fresh in your mind. If you do the assignment a few days after you finish reading, you will end up spending several minutes reacquainting yourself with what you read.

FIND LIKE-MINDED PEERS

God has created us for community. Even the busiest and most successful people in the world dedicate time to peer groups that will spur them forward. While you are in school, you should try and find someone who will sit with you in the library or several students who will form a study group—not to distract one another but to keep pushing each other toward excellence. Even introverts often like having someone they know close by, even if words aren't shared. Also, agree to edit each other's major assignments. A peer will really help you see when your writing is unclear.

Work toward an accountability relationship regarding your work. Give one another permission to do routine checks, like asking each other, "Did you go through your Greek flash cards this morning?" or "Did you stay off social media all afternoon?" There is power in accountability, and peers who are focused on productivity will push you to be productive too. This self-imposed peer pressure can serve to bolster your motivation to devote the time needed for study, rather than relying on yourself to stay accountable.

CHOOSE TO TURN OFF DISTRACTORS

In efforts to be engaged online, we often make ourselves immediately available and always ready to be interrupted. Productive people know how to set themselves up for distraction-free work. There are precious few times when there are actual emergencies that require your immediate attention. While it is true that we are frequently distracted, the truth is that we are choosing to distract ourselves, because the majority of what distracts us is entirely within our control. Here are some simple ways to stop distracting yourself.

- If you don't have the strength to cancel your Facebook account, at least turn off the notifications so that you are not getting frequent emails and updates on any of your devices. Same for Twitter and any other social media site you use.
- Turn off all notifications (including email) on your computer. Same for your mobile device.
- Change the settings of your email program so it only checks for new mail when you hit the "send/receive" button (and then stop hitting it so often!).

DISTRACTION-REDUCING APPLICATIONS

If you need a little assistance with reducing electronic distractions, some technology can actually help. Check out Freedom (freedom. to) or Saent (download.saent.com), both of which combine social media, email, or internet access blocking with pomodoro-style timing. Other options include SelfControl (selfcontrolapp.com) or Anti-Social (antisocial.80pct.com). Users of the Firefox web browser can also use the add-on LeechBlock to block social media sites for periods of time (proginosko.com/leechblock).

- Hide your phone or other mobile device in your bag so you don't see it every time it lights up.
- If you have a cell phone, turn the ringer off when you are working (and in class!).

BACK UP YOUR WORK

We have one final piece of advice regarding time management: make sure your work is backed up so you only have to do an assignment once. Only once have I (Danny) had a completed paper totally disappear on me—but what an awful feeling! If you are not safeguarding yourself by backing up your work regularly, you will at some point end up doing assignments all over again. Talk about unproductive!

Fortunately, there are some ultra-simple ways to do this. Many people carry around a portable data storage device (thumb drive), but the simplest is to install cloud storage apps, like Dropbox (dropbox.com) or Google Drive (drive.google.com). Sign up for an account, download and install the program, and you will have a folder on your computer that will be backed up to the cloud. *Every* major thing I work on is saved to one of my cloud services. Be proactive and set up a backup service before your laptop dies on you suddenly and you lose your work.

CONCLUSION

You do not want your seminary superhero name to be "The Procrastinator." To stop procrastination and move into the realm of productivity, make sure you are in charge of every single minute of your day. You need to budget your time in the same way you budget your money. Make the choice to wake up early. Make the choice to say no to time wasters. Tell yourself what to do, then do it. Always be evaluating how you are spending your time.

Honestly look at your day(s) and see if you wasted time on unimportant things. Focus on quality and productivity, and force the lazy part of yourself into submission under the one who wants to thrive at seminary.

Spending your time wisely is one of the benefits of the greater spiritual disciplines we talked about in chapter 2. Discipline in one area makes it easier to have discipline in another. For those of you who begin to practice the discipline of fasting, for example, you will essentially be commanding your appetites/hunger to submit to your will. If you are able to master your stomach, you will find that your laziness and procrastination are much easier to govern.

You are investing time and money into your education. Honor those investments and take it seriously. While most of your peers may be complaining and procrastinating, crush it by taking control of your time and being productive.

CHAPTER 6

————— 🖋 —————

Taking Care of Your Body

There is a concept in human resource management theory that people live in various domains (work, family, school, church, etc.). Each domain has a border that separates it from the others. However, because we are whole people and we travel between domains, experiences from one domain often *spill over* and *cross over* to another. When this happens, negative and positive experiences from one world impact aspects of our other worlds. As we have been saying, this means that discipline in one domain often motivates discipline in another. Productive people are disciplined people, and that discipline *should* extend from school/work to our spiritual life, and also to how we treat our bodies. Establishing healthy habits of eating, sleeping, and exercising will not only help you excel in your studies but will make you the kind of person who influences others, and one who can effectively lead churches or ministries in the future.

Our bodies, minds, and spirits are connected. While in seminary we may be tempted to neglect our bodies in favor of spending more time studying; that would be a mistake. We are whole people, and healthiness in one area of life produces fruit in the other domains of life.

EAT WELL

Hopefully by the time you get to seminary you recognize the need to eat well. Many Christians know the health dangers of smoking, but these same people may eat a fast-food diet filled with high sugar foods. I (Danny) used to live in a home with two smokers and drinkers. I could never understand the decision to waste money on cancer-causing cigarettes. Nevertheless, I ended up being an unhealthy eater for much of my life. Although making unhealthy choices regarding food did not have the same negative stigma attached to them that cigarettes did, they were not beneficial.

And while you may think it is necessary to eat well in theory, in practice it is still all too easy to live on pizza and soda. So consider the snacks that fuel your research marathons. Different seminaries have different culinary options, so make wise choices. While there are many unhealthy options, there are salad bars in almost every cafeteria! We recognize the lure of stuffing your face with quick calories, but this mentality is why many students end up gaining weight. We want you to resist temptation and realize that your brain needs good food. You aren't a teenager anymore, when it was fun to consume as much candy as possible. As an adult, it is on you to make your own choices. These include good food choices.

Students also sometimes think the only way to stay productive is to become a coffee addict or to chug energy drinks late at night to stay up. We love coffee as much as the next person, but drinking lots of coffee can be expensive and certainly isn't the best method of hydration. And if you are like us and you need cream and sugar to make your coffee palatable, you are also adding extra calories. I (Danny) have now restricted myself to one mug per day on most days, with the occasional second cup (I have learned, though, to measure out the sugar and cream). For me, and maybe you, overindulging in coffee is a stress barometer. When I start drinking multiple cups each day, it is usually a sign that I am stressed and have stretched myself too thin.

The bottom line with eating well is this: You know how much is too much, so be self-disciplined and make wise choices that will not compromise your health in the long term.

EXERCISE

I (Ben) grew up playing sports. When there was a competitive goal, sports were fun. However, now that there is no team, no game days, and no reason to continue running lines on the basketball court, there is no reason to run at all—or so I wish. Growing up, exercise may have been the means to the end of playing well, but today, exercise needs to become your *actual* end goal.

For most people, this transition doesn't come easily. Some people love exercising. We don't (but we've prayed for this wonderful gift!). Until God grants it, we work to prioritize healthy activity in our daily lives. There are seasons when life gets chaotic and it slips from our routine, but over time we work to restore the discipline. The point is that if you are waiting for exercise to become fun *before* you start excercising, then you are likely going to be waiting for awhile.

The benefits of exercise are many. One is that it gives us more energy. The analogy we like to use is that of a battery. We recharge our life battery through nourishing food, sleep, and exercise. People often mistakenly assume that exercise diminishes our energy, and it certainly feels that way when you are first attempting to get into an exercise routine. But over time, exercise actually energizes both your body and your mind. Over the past three years, I (Danny) have sought to implement a regular regimen for daily exercise. I instilled this discipline in my life for the reactive purpose of weight loss (after a lifetime of obesity) and the proactive purpose of pursuing better overall health.[1] What led to this decision to pursue exercise as a discipline was a solid two years where I could not stop falling asleep in church (which is a little embarrassing to admit). During this season I also found it difficult simply to get out of bed. However, after the first few weeks of exercise, I started to notice a lack of tiredness. When I committed myself to a solid morning routine that included exercise, the old habit of falling asleep during the sermon stopped. Getting out of bed in the morning became easier.

A regular exercise routine also naturally encourages you to make healthier choices in other areas of life. We still wrestle with old habits, but we have noticed that discipline in one area begets discipline in other areas. When we skip exercise, it is easier to justify poor eating habits. When we sleep past our morning devotions, it is eas-

---

1. A note on exercise and weight loss: While many people (particularly people who don't exercise regularly) associate exercise with losing weight, the reality is that losing weight begins in the kitchen, not in the gym. In other words, exercise, even a quite strenuous routine, cannot counteract a high-calorie diet. If you want weight loss, a regular exercise routine will compound the effects of healthy eating, but it won't usually erase the effects of poor eating.

ier to forsake budgeting in the realms of time or finances. As you discipline your time, it will be easier to discipline your devotional life, and as you discipline your devotional life, it will help to identify sinful habits (including idolizing food or entertainment). In turn, discipline in these areas will become easier.

In general, fighting with the "old man" becomes easier and easier over time. The first few months are the hardest when killing old habits or trying to begin new ones. This is why so many people give up on new pursuits after a short time. However, like the disciplines of fasting and time management, exercising is a process of teaching your body to submit to your will. And this is always a good lesson to learn no matter what area of life is being told to submit or what areas of life are feeling the pain of "dying to oneself."

How do you get exercise into your life? There are many opportunities in higher education to join intramural teams, use the gym, play sports with other students, and so on. And even if these things are not available, you still have no excuse. I (Danny) get exercise by using kettlebells without leaving my home. In times past, I exercised several times a week in my living room or office with no equipment. Body weight exercises can be done even in small rooms: these are the types of exercises I turn to when I am traveling. And if you still feel you cannot manage that, simply aim for ten thousand steps a day. Walk to school and back, take a lunchtime walk with a friend, and use a simple pedometer to make sure you hit the ten thousand mark daily.

PRACTICE REST

While Christians and Jews are familiar with the practice of Sabbath rest (even if they don't actually do it!), the idea of a consistent time of not working during the week is good for everyone. There are cycles and seasons of life, and by and large seminary means little leisure time. Still, if you've disciplined yourself to stick to your master plan, you should be able to take a day or half a day off from school work each week. Don't replace it with other work; instead, do the things you love to do: watch a movie, paint, knit, read comics, play a board game with family or friends, or take a hike. Just get your mind off assignments for a little while.

When it comes to sleep, you should be in bed between eleven and twelve each night and get six to eight hours of sleep. There is no rule that says all higher education students should sleep as little as possible. If you follow our suggestions for managing your time in the previous chapter, you won't have any reason to stay up late doing assignments anyway. In my (Danny's) early college days, I prided myself on pulling at least one all-nighter each semester. I wore it like a badge of honor. But once I was in seminary, married and with kids, that was not something I yearned to do. Yes, there were some late-night sessions, but I learned how to plan so that I wouldn't need to burn the midnight oil. This was because I was putting in the time consistently during the week and sticking to my master plan.

Some scientists and companies are also increasingly recommending naps.[2] I (Danny) frequently nap in my office. If you are the kind of person who can put your head on the desk in the library and conk out for a bit, start doing it! Naps reenergize your mind. The key to a good nap is

---

2. See, for example, Sumathi Reddy, "The Perfect Nap: Sleeping Is a Mix of Art and Science," wsj.com/articles/SB10001424127887323932 604579050990895301888.

the length—if you nap more than about twenty minutes, you will enter into a deeper sleep cycle and feel groggy when you wake up instead of refreshed. Set your alarm for twenty minutes, and practice the art of the siesta!

TAKE SHORT BREAKS

The most productive people are *not* those who glue themselves to their desk for hours on end. The most productive people hit their work hard for chunks of time, and then take breaks in between. You may want to establish a fifty-five-minute work, five-minute break routine. Some people, like professional musicians, will do ninety minutes of hard work followed by fifteen minutes of rest.

Have you ever had a deadline that you were working on, when all of a sudden a setback or tragedy hits and it takes a huge chunk of time away from you? I (Danny) have had this happen to me many times. If you were like me, many of those times *you were still able to make your deadline.* This was possible because circumstances forced you to focus in like a laser on finishing the task at hand. Everything else was shut out and you locked in to your task and attacked it with ferocity.

THE POMODORO TECHNIQUE

Scheduling intensely focused work sessions followed by short breaks is often called the Pomodoro Technique after the tomato-shaped kitchen timer used by its creator. To schedule your homework time in this manner, you can set an alarm on your computer to mark the times. If you use a Mac, you can use the program Danny uses called BreakTime (breaktimeapp.com), the previously mentioned Saent, or other pomodoro-style alarms.

Don't wait for an emergency to cause you to focus. Use disciplined scheduling to tap into your ability to focus and achieve a high level of productivity. By setting mini-deadlines throughout the day, you are forcing yourself to work hard and fast to get the reward of a break. If you do this type of scheduling, you will begin to challenge yourself to get certain amounts done before your break comes. In the effort to hit these mini-targets, you will force yourself to focus and not be distracted.

CONCLUSION

Several years ago, I (Ben) was preparing to teach a new course for the following fall semester. The title of the course was "The Life of Leaders." Essentially it was a course exploring the great leaders of church history and asking the question, "What did they do that made them worth following?" Most of the leaders explored were known primarily as theologians, missionaries, or evangelists, who led others throughout their ministry with great followings. I selected such leaders as Martin Luther, Dietrich Bonhoeffer, Jonathan Edwards, Amy Carmichael, William Carey, Adoniram Judson, D. L. Moody, and Billy Graham to explore in more depth.

Going in to the course I had a crisis of competency. I started asking the question, "Am I a leader worth following?" I began to look at my life while I was looking at the lives of these great leaders. I asked the questions of myself that I was asking about the men and women who were going to be the true teachers of the class. Through this time of reflection I recognized five areas of my life where indulgence reigned (over-eating, over-spending, and over-sleeping, while under-excercising both my spiritual life and my body).[3] The area that seemed most urgent was in the realm of what I ate. I have always had a high metabolism and didn't struggle with weight, so this wasn't an obvious struggle. But as I considered what I saw, I recognized that the problem was with my *appetite* for food—good food, nice food, rich food. And while it didn't necessarily show up on my waist, it showed up in my heart.

During this season I started to learn how to rein in the "spoiled child" that lived in my stomach.[4] It was also during this season that I recognized how interdependent discipline truly was. As I reined in what I ate, I recognized that my spending habits got better. And as I disciplined myself in these areas, I recognized the spiritual battle that was taking place (because in reality, I was struggling with an inward gluttony). Thus the battle, while somewhat physical, was significantly spiritual, and I needed the sustenance that feasting on the Word provided. Each of these areas of discipline aided in the transformation of the other areas that the Lord was revealing to me as weak points in my leadership.

So in the same way that you should continue your spiritual growth and cultivate holy habits, you need to continue to take care of your body. Your life is a gift; you are fearfully and wonderfully made (Ps 139:14). Taking care of your body is part of your stewardship as a Christian leader. If you are going into the ministry, you will essentially spend the rest of your life saying with Paul, "Follow me as I follow Christ" (1 Cor 11:1). What type of person do you want to replicate in the pews of your church? Do you

---

3. A book I found later on in life, but would have been helpful in identifying these overindulgences, is Marshall Segal, ed., *Killjoys: The Seven Deadly Sins* (Minneapolis: Desiring God, 2015).

4. See Foster, *Celebration of Discipline,* 57.

want to encourage your congregation to spend their lives following you as you follow Christ if you spend your life as an overindulging workaholic? To borrow a phrase Paul liked to use: By no means! Our goal is to equip the saints for the work of the ministry (Eph 4:11–12), and part of doing this is to equip them toward holiness *and* wisdom.

These are lessons you may continually have to relearn and reapply. Learning to be disciplined in taking care of your body is not a lesson learned once, and thus your trajectory is set forever. It is easier in some ways the second time around because you "know" the lessons, but it is also harder because you "know" how hard it is to deny your flesh that cries out for more. This is why the *journey* metaphor for the Christian life is so helpful. Health in mind, body, and spirit is not a destination we reach, but a road we travel.

CHAPTER 7

Juggling Ministry with
Your Studies

G one are the days when seminary students were solely
focused on their education, tucked in the halls of the
school wearing their academic regalia with little else than
study clamoring for their attention. Today many students
have to balance their studies with their roles as full-time
pastors, part-time assistants, or lay leaders within their
church. Even those who are not already engaged in active
ministry will usually be involved in field education as part
of their degree program.

It is completely understandable for students to struggle with balancing study and practice. After all, you feel
called to ministry. You want to pour yourself into people.
And more can always be done. More hurting people can
use your encouragement, another program can be run,
another phone call can be made. It is very common for

students to face temptations to overexert or overcommit, which leads to burnout.

In a meeting one day, a mentor of Ben's recalled writing in his Bible as a young seminary student, "I'd rather burn out for the Lord than rust out!" Reflecting on that memory nearly fifty years later, he regretted such a perspective and encouraged all who were in the room to do neither! Burning out and rusting out are both ways to ruin one's legacy. Neither one is the calling that God has placed on the leaders of his church. Rather, as a seminarian you are called to live in the tension between studying and ministering. This chapter is about managing those two responsibilities well.

DON'T SEPARATE SEMINARY FROM MINISTRY

Sometimes students are tempted to not juggle their ministry and schooling at all, but opt for jumping into full-time ministry. This can lead to them leaving the seminary too early and being ill-prepared for the task that lies ahead. We encourage you to fan the flame of enthusiasm, but leaving before you are finished is generally unwise.[1] How many of us want our pilots to finish flight school before they lift us off the ground? How many of us want our pharmacists to finish their chemistry coursework

---

1. We recognize that for a select few, advanced education or advanced education at this point in life may not be God's plan for your ministry. At times he has called leaders to leave early, but we contend that this is the exception and not the rule. Preparation in ministry is *necessary* for the task that lays before us all. For as many as have left early and succeeded, there are likely many more who left before they were ready spiritually, academically, and practically, with their ministry (and family and testimony) quite often suffering for it.

before they create our medication? How many of us want our surgeons to finish medical school and their surgical rotation before they cut us open?

The church father Gregory the Great said that the care of souls is the art of arts.[2] We want those who are called to the health of souls to finish their course of study so they are ready for the challenges that lie ahead. Do not fall for the trap of dreaming about the glorious day when you will get into "real ministry." Ministry is simply equipping the saints to do the work of the ministry (Eph 4:11–12). Thus, if you are involved in learning, you are in the ministry of equipping. This will eventually mature into your ability to equip others.

Furthermore, if you are involved in spending time with people, praying with them and for them, and challenging them to think deeply about the Word of God, then you are in ministry. Some of your fellow seminarians will have a crisis of faith during their studies, some will face the death of a loved one, some will face financial pressures, and some will question their calling and their identity as adopted heirs of God. Encouraging and equipping people in contexts such as these is ministry. So invest in the maturation of others for the sake of their calling and yours. Do not go through this season of life waiting for ministry to start; it already has. You are charged to minister wherever you are.

Don't separate your study from your call to ministry. Succeeding in your seminary studies should be one of your main goals during this season of your life. Ministry is not something that magically happens on graduation. Ministry is something that is cultivated and dis-

---

2. See Gregory the Great, *The Book of Pastoral Rule*, Popular Patristics Series 34 (Crestwood, NY: St. Vladimir's Seminary Press, 2007), 30.

ciplined into your life *as you go through* life. In the Great Commission, Christ charges his disciples, "In your going ... make disciples" (Matt 28:19-20). In this context of active living, we are to do ministry. Similarly, in the family discipleship passage of Deuteronomy 6, parents are told to teach their children when they sit at home, when they walk by the way, when they lie down at night, and when they rise in the morning. This is ministry that is done in the context of living. Practice the skills of ministry right now, starting today, not waiting for tomorrow or for graduation. Just like we don't want you to leave school without finalizing your preparation, we don't want you to wait to practice ministry for graduation. Separating study from ministry tends to lead to a theology of discipleship where discipleship is studied, learned, and theologized about more than it is practiced.

SEMINARY IS A
TIME TO INVEST IN RELATIONSHIPS

Ministry is inherently relational. Ben remembers a professor once quipping about his dream job: a prestigious professorship at an institution in the United Kingdom that required no teaching or interaction with students. Positions like this one are the exception. While some ministry roles have more interaction and some have less, the point is that in order to prepare yourself for ministry, you need to prepare yourself for people.

We want you to be sensitive to your friendships and encourage you to always value people. If seminary takes you out of the world, then you are learning how to do theology in a vacuum. Theology is meant to be lived and practiced in relationship. Here are some particular relationships to invest in while you are in seminary.

Existing Relationships

When you begin your seminary journey, the same difficulties you can have with your spouse may also occur with friends and extended family. In some cases, former friendships will not be as appealing as they once were. Friendships built on superficiality are being replaced by friendships built on faith and the deeper things of God. Friendships of common likes and dislikes are now transitioning to friendships surrounding calling, vision, and values.

Proceed wisely with friendships from the past. Recognize that you have a limited amount of time in life, and the little time you have will need to be budgeted. Friendships built around online RPGs, the latest version of Halo, or binge watching the last season of your favorite TV show will almost certainly change. You no longer have time for these hobbies (except on rare occasions or during breaks in school). Prepare close friends for the changes in your schedule and your life. Explain to them why you are pursuing this education and where you think God is calling you. This may even be an opportunity to share the gospel with a friend who has always remained uninterested or is on the fringes of faith. Explain what the "cost of discipleship" is demanding of you and how you are responding in obedience. This action can speak loudly!

Relationships with Fellow Students

As you prepare for ministry, be deliberate about being enriched by the array of fellow students you will meet at seminary. God calls a wide variety of people to ministry; seek to learn from them. Respect older students who have more life experience than you. Honor the vigor, zeal, and energy of younger students. Deal respectfully with students you disagree with. Learn from fellow students who are gifted in knowledge and understanding. Share your story and listen to the stories of others, especially international students or students in different ministry environments.

You are rubbing shoulders with people who are on the same team. You are not entering a competitive environment where one-upmanship may ensure that you secure a job in a limited pool. You are not in the rat race of private-sector work—you are a fellow builder of God's kingdom. You and your fellow students are in this together. Their success is your success. You are in a process of being molded by God. People come to seminary from various backgrounds and with an assortment of colorful stories. You have a chance not only to learn the deep truth of God but also to bless and be a blessing while pursuing your education.

In particular, go out of your way to cultivate friendships with international students. In Ben's role in his seminary, he has been thoroughly impressed with the international students moving to the United States. They have given up much to relocate to a strange world. Some students leave behind families for a season. Others bring their families, which doubles the newness experienced in the North American culture. These students have a story that has brought them to this time and place. Learn their story! Invite them to share a meal in your home. Most cultures outside North America are much more communal that we are. Thus, it is likely that the international students around you are waiting for and expecting someone to show them how to do this seminary thing while living in North America. So step out and invite them to church, take them to the grocery store, and learn from their commitment and dedication to following Christ.

Likewise, if you are an international student, you have much to offer your peers and professors. Take time to teach those of us who are from the individualistic West what it looks like to grow in community. You have a story and a background that North Americans need to hear. We need to hear the stories of how those in your country are soaking up the Word of God and seeking biblical training. We also need to hear the stories of the hardships and possibly even the persecution that Christians are facing in your country. These stories will help us to see needs and to become more globally minded in our faith.

When I (Ben) was teaching an introductory course for new seminary students, we spent a week covering a theology of mission. I paused in my lecture and asked a student from India how much it would cost for one of his American classmates to be trained and sent to his home country. The Indian student gave a figure (which was more than I make in a month). Then I asked, "How much would it take for your classmates to send *you* back home to minister in the same way?" The student replied, "About 20 percent of what it would cost for an American." This is not only fiscally responsible, but it is a philosophy of missions that equips national pastors to pastor in their national church.

So take time to get to know the international students around you. Bond with them, pray with them, and prepare your heart together so that you are their best supporter as they go back to the mission field that is their home. Maybe one day you can support them in their calling through your future church and ministry by being a sender and an equipper.

Relationships in the Church

Christ loves the church, and thus we need to love the church. Christ gave his life for the church, and as his servants and under shepherds, we have the joyful role of cherishing it. However, seminary is focused on discussing and theologizing about the ideal church. This means that what we find in actual churches never lives up to the ideals we see in our classes. This is because the church is made up of people and not just words. These people who make up the church are like us—sinful, selfish, and broken. The actual churches in our communities will not always live up to the picture we might be creating in our minds. In spite of this, each imperfect congregation of sinners is part of the bride of Christ, and therefore you have a role to play in her sanctification. Embrace this role and find ways to serve the church out of obedience to Christ and reverence for his name. There are two pieces of advice with regard to the church that we especially think seminarians should consider as they prepare for ministry.

First, to borrow a line from Joshua Harris, stop dating the church![3] Too many seminary students "date" different churches, waiting to find the church that will (a) hire them, (b) set them up to be hired, or (c) fulfill their immediate needs. Some who date the church do so by accident. For instance, this type of seminarian thinks that the church is a family and because of the transient nature of a seminary subculture, each year (or semester) brings new roommates and thus a "new family." Therefore, each year (or semester) they attend a new church. Church is to be a family; however, this doesn't mean you bail on your cur-

---

3. Joshua Harris, *Stop Dating the Church! Fall in Love with the Family of God* (Colorado Springs: Multnomah Books, 2004).

rent family whenever a new family moves in next door.[4] Find a church for your seminary experience, and commit to it.

Another type of student who dates the church is the one who allegedly wants to sample church leadership and ministry methodology, but in reality wants to keep the church at arm's length so they don't have to make a commitment to an imperfect group of people. Because seminary students are studying ecclesiology, they have grand ideas of how they would or could perfect the local church. They attend a church until they recognize it is not perfect, and then they dump that church for another one down the street. This attitude is born out of the consumerism of Western culture, and it leads to perpetual immaturity. If you are tempted to be a serial church dater, give yourself one month to find a church; then commit to that church for the duration of your seminary experience or until God *clearly* moves you elsewhere.

In his classic text written from the demonic perspective of Screwtape, C. S. Lewis gives some enlightening advice to his junior-demon nephew Wormwood on this subject:

> My dear Wormwood,
>
> You mentioned casually in your last letter that the patient has continued to attend one church, and one only, since he was converted, and that he is not wholly pleased with it. May I ask what you are about? Why have I no report on the causes of his fidelity to the parish church? Do you realize that

---

4. On this topic we recommend reading Joseph H. Hellerman, *When the Church Was a Family: Recapturing Jesus' Vision for Authentic Christian Community* (Nashville: B&H, 2009).

unless it is due to indifference it is a very bad thing? Surely you know that if a man can't be cured of churchgoing, the next best thing is to send him all over the neighbourhood looking for the church that "suits" him until he becomes a taster or connoisseur of churches.[5]

Instead of looking for a perfect church, look for a church in which you can serve. When we say "serve," we do not mean in a grand/important/significant way (that *may* come after consistent investment). Instead, serve by parking cars, playing dodgeball, teaching kids how to put on the armor of God, teaching teens how to battle their flesh, teaching the older adults about the christological themes found in Paul's writings, or mowing the yards of people who can't do it themselves. All of these are acts of service. Some may feel more personally fulfilling than others, but all are important. They are ways of obeying Christ's command to serve others, and reflect his service of us through the incarnation. Purposefully learning the art of serving now will equip you for your life of ministry later. It will also help you to guard against the cynicism that is rampant in seminary.[6]

Second, reject cynicism and superiority. While you are in seminary, some of you will attend large churches with well-run and well-staffed ministries, but there are many more churches with a country pastor who serves bi-vocationally. Whatever church you may be in, keep any attitudes of superiority in check and cultivate a humble attitude and a servant's heart. Don't drop knowledge

---

5. C. S. Lewis, *The Screwtape Letters*, annotated edition (San Francisco: HarperCollins, 2013), 93.
6. On this, Timothy Gombis has some great insights in "Advice for Seminoids," timgombis.com/2012/10/11/advice-for-seminoids.

bombs on your church family; instead, be a gentle shepherd that teaches the Word with respect for it and for them. This is not to say you can never talk to people about seminary and what you are learning, but be mindful of where they are in their own faith journey and recognize that you are learning at a different level. Attitudes of cynicism and superiority are why there is sometimes a negative view of seminaries in local churches; the old joke that seminaries are really "cemeteries" where a person's faith goes to die is alive and well.

Relationships with Professors

One of the best ways to prepare for ministry is to cultivate relationships with your professors. Jonathan Edwards said, "There are two ways of representing and recommending true religion and virtue to the world, which God hath made use of: the one is by doctrine and precept, the other is by instance and example."[7] The lives of your professors should be a modern incarnation of this instance and example. However, as professors, we know that we are not perfect. We have not accomplished sanctification, but we have been on this journey for years, and the Lord, in his grace, saw fit to place us in our roles at our institutions. Learn from us! Watch us at church, watch us when we pray, watch us when we interact with our families. If you watch long enough and close enough, you will eventually see something we regret, but hopefully we will also be quick to confess and you can learn from that as well. Most of your professors are bright and could have done a number of things with their life and talents. We chose this

---

7. Jonathan Edwards, *The Diary and Journal of David Brainerd* (Carlisle, PA: Banner of Truth Trust, 2007), xli.

particular vocation because we love the Lord, we love his Word, and we love teaching it to you, our students.

On a related note, we challenge you to embrace the time you have in seminary by involving yourself in the life of your institution as much as you can. Not only will you benefit from the community, but you will also be a benefit to the community. Your professors are wise men and women who have spent years studying in their fields and also have often spent years in ministry in the church and seminary. They are called to equip future Christian leaders, and their role is to invest in you and your peers. You can be the aloof student who sits in the back of the class and rarely says a word, or you can be the student who is known personally by the faculty.

When you graduate, we will write your recommendation letters. Some of the letters we have written were generic because sometimes all we remember about a student is that they sat in the back of our classes and got a B. Other recommendation letters are specific, heartfelt, and persuasive. These are for the students who we have known outside of class and not just in lectures. Let us see you involved in community life, in class, and in the community worship times. You will be the better for it, and your experience will be much richer if you do.

Relationships with Ministry Mentors

Just as you learn from your professors, part of preparing for ministry is learning from ministry mentors. Just as Timothy was discipled by Paul, you also need a mentor to help you understand some of the practical aspects of ministry. Years ago, I (Ben) had the opportunity to go to lunch with a decorated two-star general. As I was peppering him with questions about life and leadership, he recalled a recent conversation with his mentor. I stopped him there: "You have a mentor?!" Not only did he have a mentor at that time, but he also talked about the importance of mentorship in his life over the years. This West Point graduate had climbed the ladder of the military to a very selective level and still recognized the importance of mentorship. Mentorship is not just something that you pursue while you are young in your career or ministry. It is something you pursue as long as you want to grow and be shaped for greater effectiveness in ministry.

For most seminarians, their ministry mentor will be their supervising pastor in their church. For those who are the pastors of a church, it may be a deacon, elder, or other denominational leader in their church. This relationship can be a great one, but it requires teachability and a clear definition of what is expected. As we stated earlier, proper balance is needed; make sure you are giving the right energy to the right domains of your life. Thus, whether you are a full-time pastor or a full-time student, you need to give your full-time calling the priority. As much as you may want to increase the amount of work you are doing in your part-time role, you cannot let yourself get overburdened with work that is not your primary calling.

To make sure this doesn't happen, have an honest conversation with your mentor(s) about the expectations of your ministry role. Be up front from the beginning. For those of you who are full-time students, explain that success in your studies is one of your top priorities, and ask them to help you guard your time so that your part-time ministry doesn't end up consuming all of your school time. If you've explained yourself well, they will not only keep you accountable but will play defense for you, helping to deflect requests for your time, and hold back from overburdening you themselves.

You also need to get clear on what your supervisor is expecting from you in terms of meetings and church functions. Are you expected at every church meeting? Every prayer meeting? All services? If you are expected to be at every meeting and church function, this needs to be recognized as part of the hours that you put in. To stay focused on your studies, you may want to excuse yourself from some of these, but you need the support of your supervisor and/or the church leadership for this.

Relationships with Those You Mentor

Who are you mentoring? If you can't answer this question, you need to create a plan for practicing what you are studying. If the great commission is to make disciples, and you are going to spend the next few years studying how to make disciples, it only makes sense that you would put what you are studying into practice now. One of the temptations for seminarians is to think that the best way to *do* discipleship is to study *about* discipleship. Studying is important (and why we have committed our lives to teaching others), but the best way to study discipleship is to disciple others.

Learn to practice now while you have mentors around you who are able to answer any questions you might have while in the disciple-making process. If you are unsure how to go about this, find a high-school or college student who needs a friend, find a first-year student who needs a prayer partner, find an elderly widow in your church, or even find an outspoken atheist on the campus of the local college. Ask them if you can talk to them about Jesus on a weekly basis if you buy them coffee. Find someone to pour into so that you are using the life-giving water that you are taking in. As you pour this water out, you will find that you are personally being refreshed. When you store up the water without pouring it out, you will build up stale water that becomes lukewarm and even bitter (or cynical).

PRACTICAL TIPS FOR JUGGLING STUDY AND MINISTRY

If you are pursuing ministry practice as well as academic study, then you are busy. The old joke goes that there is no such thing as serving "part-time" in the church—just full-time service on part-time pay.

This busyness doesn't go away upon graduation. It will change and grow with you as your life and your abilities grow. Instead of writing a paper each week and submitting it to a professor, it is likely that you are instead going to present orally in front of a group what you have studied all week. Instead of hiding behind a screen or a paper that is read out of your sight, you are now looking in the eyes of your recipients as you preach and teach. This is a joy and a blessing! You are now in the position to share the water from the well that you have been digging. In order to get to this position, we have a few practical suggestions to help you balance the many tasks that make up your journey of preparation.

1. **Be realistic.** If you are a full-time student, you simply cannot pour yourself fully into your studies *and* your ministry or practicum. You may desire to start new programs and also ace your Greek exam. For some of you this is realistic; you may have a background in Greek or you may be one of those leaders who easily understands systems. Others may need to choose where best to invest their time. Your desire to start new programs and new ministries is a great thing, but you cannot do it all. If you launch a new program that requires a lot of your time, your studies will suffer. You know yourself

(more than we do), so you should know when to pull on the reins and hold yourself back when needed. The time will come when you will begin new and exciting ministry—but in most cases, seminary is not the time.

2. **Be stingy.** Choosing to work on a degree means choosing to invest your time to succeed in your studies. If you are in ministry part time while studying full time, then ministry will inevitably creep into your study time. Be on guard against the pressures for one more meeting or one more activity.

Being stingy with your time does *not* mean that you lessen your effort in your ministry. Rather, you need to guard your time from being taken up by non-essentials. If there is a meeting or church function that is above the time you are paid for, ask whether you need to be there. Don't worry about what others might think; most will understand that studying takes a lot of your time. If you are unsure, ask your ministry supervisor, "Is it 100 percent necessary that I be there?" If they say no, tell them you won't be there. If you have a supportive supervisor, they will understand. In general, you should establish a not-to-do list for your church work, talk it through with your supervisor or church leadership, and then stick to it.

In short, you should say no as often as you can without shirking responsibility. We have to do this all the time as professors, and we still find it painful. However, books don't get written, lesson plans don't get created, and discipleship doesn't take place simultaneously. We have to budget our time and energy and be willing to say no to things that don't make the cut. Saying no to unnecessary things means that you can spend the proper amount of time and energy on your studies as well as the ministry you are actually there to do. Giving yourself permission to offer a firm no means allowing yourself to commit to your best yes. Spread yourself too thin, and nothing will be done well.

3. **Find someone to hold you accountable.** These are people who will help you with these decisions and help you stay committed to decisions you have already made. Rehoboam wisely asked for counsel from his father's advisors, but he foolishly disregarded their counsel and instead listened to his sycophantic friends (1 Kgs 12:6–8). We firmly believe that if you will look, there are many wise advisors around you who will be willing to be a sounding board and counselors throughout your seminary and post-seminary experience. Ask your professors, your ministry supervisor, or your spouse to help hold you accountable for your time and efforts. Your fellow seminarians are also great accountability partners as they understand the current pressures you are facing in the classroom as well as in your ministry context. Open and honest communication with your professors and ministry supervisor can often be just the wise counsel you need. You are not in ministry alone, and at seminary you have plenty of experienced people around you to draw from.

4. **Be ready for hard decisions.** There will be times when you really want to be involved in something at church but you don't have the time for it. Odds are you are the only one feeling this way. There aren't usually people at the church judging you and won-

dering what you do with your time. Make the hard decision to stay out of things and be okay with it.

Conversely, sometimes you will need to make the hard decision to drop an assignment, not complete that reading, or even drop a course because of unforeseen circumstances in your ministry. If you have carefully thought about it, sought counsel from friends, your ministry leaders, and professors, and feel that the ministry must take precedence over your studies, then be okay with this hard decision too. You will be no use to anyone if you burn out because you tried to do too much.

CONCLUSION

We commend you for accepting God's call to pursue preparation for ministry. If the church is Christ's bride, and we believe it is, then it is a high and holy calling to lead his bride as part of your vocation. Preparation for this role requires wisdom and diligence. What we have covered here is only the beginning, but we hope it has provided a basic framework for thinking about juggling your study commitments with your ministry commitments. Seminary is not a time-out from investing in ministry; it is the laboratory for whole-hearted, experimental ministry practice. So challenge yourself to pursue what Christ has laid before you. Do not think that this is something that can be done later in life. (It can be done later in life, but why wait?) Instead, take full advantage of the opportunities you have before you for intentional investment in kingdom ministry.

PART 3

STUDY SKILLS AND TOOLS

CHAPTER 8

Research Skills

The saying that "a carpenter is only as good as his tools" is true in all of life. Professional golfers, for example, arm themselves with top-notch clubs and gear. But more than that, they work hard to learn how to use those tools to the best of their ability. Like any pro out there, they practice their skills. For your life as a student, you need to arm yourself with both skills and tools in order to be successful. Learn a few core skills, and you will not only survive but thrive at seminary. Know how to use a few tools, and you'll be the envy of your fellow students. This chapter and the next will help you acquire the skills of research, reading, and writing. The final chapter is about acquiring a few of the right tools.

GET TO KNOW THE LIBRARY

The first step in learning the skill of research is becoming familiar with the library. Every paper you write should involve at least one trip there. While you can find a lot online, particularly journal articles, books and book chapters still largely require a trip to the library. Don't let laziness prevent you from finding the best sources for a paper.

The library is a big place, and you are wise to take some time to understand where materials are and how the system works. During your orientation week you may receive a library tour. Even after that, during the first weeks of the semester, you may want to get an appointment with the librarian or another knowledgeable staff member. Get them to explain to you the online catalog system. Ask them how to access online journals. Ask what the process is for getting something your library may not have. When you are ready to launch into your first paper in a particular field, seek out any specialists your library might have for that area of research. Ask them how to find good sources on a topic, and find out what online database(s) you should use when looking for quality sources. A portion of your tuition goes toward the library—it is meant to be a huge reservoir of resources for you. So get the training to make use of it!

Learning the skill of research takes time, and librarians have put in that time. If they have a master's or other advanced degree in library science, they spent additional years beyond their first degree learning how to discern, locate, and use information in the library. Rely on them to help you develop your research skills. Take advantage of library research seminars. This may sound as exciting as learning how to type properly, but trust me when I say that it will pay off handsomely in the end.

PRIMARY AND SECONDARY SOURCES
In addition to getting to know the library, knowing the different types of academic literature will help you sharpen

your research skills. Sources you will use fall into two broad categories: primary sources and secondary sources.

Primary sources are the literature or artifacts that are the focus of a paper, and secondary sources contain other authors' discussions of the primary source. For example, say you are writing an exegetical paper on Romans 3:23. In that paper, Romans is your primary source. In studying for your paper, you read and subsequently make use of Martin Luther's *Commentary on Romans*. In this essay, Martin Luther's work is a secondary source, while Romans is the primary source. But let's say that in the same semester in your Reformation Theology class, you are doing an essay on the theology of Martin Luther. In this essay, any writing by Martin Luther, including his *Commentary on Romans*, would be considered a primary source.

This means that for research papers on the Bible, the Bible is a primary source. But the Bible is not the only primary source that can be used in a biblical studies paper; other ancient sources can be used as well. For instance, if a passage from the Apocrypha, a passage from the Dead Sea Scrolls, or an archaeological artifact are discussed or quoted in a paper, these are also primary sources.

The broad category of secondary sources can be further divided into publication types. *Monographs* are books on a single topic; they can either have a single author or a group of coauthors. There are several academic publishers that publish the bulk of academic monographs in theology. Your seminary (or a nearby university) library is usually your best source for academic monographs. Monographs published by academic publishers have typically gone through an editorial process, and the authors are scholars who engage in serious academic research. You should be careful before using a non-academic monograph that you find in a local bookstore or from an online retailer. If it is from a trade publisher, or even self-published, this type of book will not usually be considered a good source for an academic paper.

A *book chapter* is an essay written by a scholar that has been collected with other essays and published in an edited book. These books of collected essays are also published by academic publishers and go through a similar process of editing and review, making them another valuable source for your research.

Journal articles are written typically by a single author and are published in a journal. Whereas book chapters are usually gathered around a single topic, a journal will have numerous articles that address different topics. Academic journal articles are highly respected because they have a peer-review process, and academic journals are typically where original research is first published. Consult with your professor to find out which ones he or she thinks are best.

It is important to recognize the difference between a *magazine article* and a journal article (both journals and magazines are sometimes called *periodicals*). A magazine article is a popular-level piece typically by a single author. It is not generally concerned with providing all sides of a discussion or carefully noting sources, and has not gone through a peer-review process. In some instances, like when discussing current trends or issues in the contemporary church, magazine articles such as those in *Christianity Today* will be acceptable, but be careful not to overuse magazine articles and consult your professor beforehand.

Bible commentaries contain verse-by-verse or section-by-section discussion of books of the Bible. They can range in scope from a single volume that covers the entire Bible to multi-volume series that have a volume devoted to each book of the Bible. Commentaries fall broadly into three categories: devotional, pastoral, and technical or academic. For your seminary research, you want to mostly confine yourself to academic commentaries, as they will engage in the discussions of Scripture that are happening in the academy.

Bible dictionaries are not like conventional dictionaries, which contain short definitions of words or terms. A Bible dictionary is more similar to an encyclopedia, since it contains longer articles. Depending on the comprehensiveness of the Bible dictionary, the articles may be short and succinct, or quite comprehensive. In most cases, academic research papers should avoid citing Bible dictionaries, since the entries do not usually represent original research. However, they are excellent places to begin to familiarize yourself with a new topic before exploring other secondary sources on the issue.

Lexicons are dictionaries of the primary languages (Greek, Hebrew, Aramaic). There are two or three standard lexicons for each language that your professors will approve for use, so consult with them to ensure that you are using high-quality lexicons.

Theological dictionaries contain studies on individual words or word groups in the primary languages and include reflection on the theological usage and significance of a word. Think of theological dictionaries as a commentary on the lexicon. I have always found theological dictionaries to be very rich in content when doing studies on individual words.

A *web source* is an online article or blog post that usually has had no official peer review. These are largely opinion pieces and are not considered to be proper academic sources for research in seminary. For the most part, avoid web sources for academic papers. It is important to note, however, that many, if not most, journals are now published online as well as in print. If you find a journal article online through your library website, this is not considered a web source.

You need to understand the distinction between primary and secondary sources because the goal of a research paper is to enter into the conversation that is going on in the secondary sources in order to better understand and interpret the primary sources. Your professor will want to see evidence that you are working with both primary and secondary sources. Very often, student essays become unbalanced. One student may focus almost solely on the primary sources, quoting a lot of primary material and recording their own interpretation on those sources, without going to the secondary sources to see what other researchers have thought. Another student may quote and cite secondary sources at length without consulting and working through the primary sources. Both of these students are making use of sources in an unbalanced way.

A RULE OF THUMB FOR SOURCES

For academic papers, the bulk of your grade is based on the quality of your research and your presentation of it. If your paper is not built on quality research, you will not produce a quality paper. I (Danny) have graded many research papers that had excellent grammar and a coherent and logical flow, but their bibliography was abysmal. What read like an A paper was researched like a D paper. No matter how well you write, your professor will spot poor research and grade accordingly.

If you follow a simple source rule that I teach my students, you will be able to produce work of sufficient quality. The rule is *one source per page, plus one*. For a ten-page paper, aim for *at minimum* 11 sources. For a twenty-page paper, aim for *at minimum* twenty-one sources. Aiming for this number of quality sources *and actually making use of them* will signal to your professor that you took the time to find an adequate number of sources to research your topic. Please note that I use the word *adequate*. Next time you read an academic journal article, you will note many more sources used than this rule of thumb. So if you want to be beyond adequate, do what the pros do!

In addition to following the above rule, you should also make one-third of your sources academic journal articles. Although they are not bestsellers, academic journals are where the latest research first gets published (which means you will also want to pay attention to the date of the article if you are looking for current research on the topic). Some of this research then makes its way into books and book chapters—often many years later. So when you use journal articles for your research, you signal to your professor that you are engaging in the latest discussion of the topic.

If you are working on a master's or doctoral thesis, this source rule does not apply. When you write a thesis, you are expected to become an expert in your topic. This means your research needs to be a lot more exhaustive, and your source count should be much higher than the "one source per page plus one" rule.

SEEK OUT QUALITY SOURCES

Now that you know how many sources to cite, you may be wondering exactly *how* to find these quality sources. Fortunately, there is a very simple way to find quality sources and build your bibliography quickly. You can go to several places.

Dictionary Articles

As mentioned above, biblical and theological dictionaries summarize and introduce a particular topic in as concise a manner as possible. Because of this, we recommend that you try to start the research process for *every* paper you write by reading dictionary articles. Reading a dictionary article will provide you with a quick and comprehensive

---

DICTIONARY RECOMMENDATIONS

We recommend the following Bible dictionaries. While we only list the *Dictionary of Jesus and the Gospels* here, all volumes in the InterVarsity Press "black dictionary" series are useful.

Alexander, T. Desmond, and Brian S. Rosner, eds. *New Dictionary of Biblical Theology*. Downers Grove, IL: IVP Academic, 2000.

Cross, F. L., and Elizabeth A. Livingstone, eds. *The Oxford Dictionary of the Christian Church*. Oxford; New York: Oxford University Press, 2005.

Di Berardino, Angelo. *Encyclopedia of Ancient Christianity*. Downers Grove, IL: IVP Academic, 2014.

Freedman, David Noel, Gary A. Herion, David F. Graf, John David Pleins, and Astrid B. Beck, eds. *The Anchor Yale Bible Dictionary*. New York: Doubleday, 1992.

Green, Joel B., Jeannine K. Brown, and Nicholas Perrin, eds. *Dictionary of Jesus and the Gospels, Second Edition*. Downers Grove, IL: IVP Academic, 2013.

Hart, Trevor A., and Richard Bauckham. *The Dictionary of Historical Theology*. Carlisle, Cumbria, U.K.: Paternoster Press, 2000.

McKim, Donald K., ed. *Dictionary of Major Biblical Interpreters*. Downers Grove, IL; Nottingham, England: InterVarsity Press, 2007.

overview of your subject. After reading several dictionary articles, you will begin to feel you have a general understanding of the topic, and this will provide you with a solid base from which to begin reading further.

Dictionary articles also provide a basic bibliography on the subject at the end of each article. Flipping to the end of the article will usually provide you with a good bibliography immediately. If you make note of the sources in the bibliographies from different dictionaries on the same topic, you will likely already have more sources than you can handle. If you end up with more sources than you can realistically track down, prioritize sources in more recent dictionaries. A dictionary article written in 1950 may be very valuable, but its bibliography will not have more recent scholarship on the issue. Dictionary articles apply best to biblical studies, theology, and church history. Ask your professors which dictionaries they recommend you use, or see the sidebar for our recommendations.

Commentaries

Commentaries apply primarily to exegesis papers and papers related to biblical theology. Commentaries, like dictionary articles, attempt to give a summary of a particular issue—only this time the issue is the proper meaning of a particular section of the Bible. Some commentaries are more comprehensive than others; it largely depends on the commentary series. To determine which commentaries are the best for the passage you are looking at, we recommend asking your professor or consulting the website bestcommentaries.com. Take care when choosing a commentary, because not all are created equal. For research papers, academic commentaries are what you need to use, as they engage with the academic discussion of the biblical book. Bestcommentaries.com is helpful in this regard, since it tags commentaries as technical, pastoral, or devotional.

Like dictionary articles, each commentary will include a bibliography. Some commentaries have a selected bibliography at the end of a passage; others have all their sources listed in the general bibliography for the whole book. Even without a selected bibliography, you can gather sources by taking a good look at the footnotes to see what is cited. Consult a few top-notch academic commentaries, and you will have a wealth of sources to use. Something to also keep in mind is the age of the commentary. The newer the commentary, the more up-to-date the bibliography.

Book Bibliographies

If you are researching a particular topic and have access to either a book or a book chapter that covers the topic, then the bibliography and footnotes of these sources will provide you with a wealth of possible sources for your own research. Like the above methods, you will need to judge for yourself based on the title if the source is worth your time (see chapter 9 for more on this).

ATLA Serials

The above suggestions will usually yield enough sources that you will not need to go hunting for more (unless you are working on a thesis or a topic not well covered by a dictionary). If your bibliography for your paper is still thin, *ATLAS* is the place to go. *ATLA* (American Theological Library Association) Serials is an online collection of journals for the study of religion. This includes not only Bible and theology, but the area of practical theology and even other religions as well. This database is a subscription service, and every good seminary library has access to it. *ATLAS* makes every part of its sources searchable, so you can search by keyword to find journal sources.

Not only can *ATLAS* help you harvest for quality sources, but you also have access to full journal articles. You can download the PDF of many articles and book reviews directly from *ATLAS*. Another option for finding sources is the *ATLA Religion Database*, which only contains bibliographic records, not the full text.

Once you've compiled a list of sources from the above places, you still need to go and actually collect them. This is where your library skills will come into play. Use your library's catalog to determine if your library has the source, or download the source directly if you find it through *ATLAS*. If a source you need is not in your library or on *ATLAS*, ask your librarian for help. You may be able to get it via interlibrary loan.

CITING SOURCES

Citation is the method by which you indicate what books or articles you are quoting or referencing in your paper. Professors always want you to properly cite sources that you use in an assignment. It may seem tedious (and it sometimes is), but do not neglect it. Find out how your professor wants it done. Some schools will have a standard method adopted for every class in the seminary, or

ATLAS TUTORIAL

ATLAS is so important to understand and use that I (Danny) have created a video tutorial on how to use it: "Finding Academic Resources for Theological Studies Utilizing ATLAS." You can view the tutorial at this link: atlas.DannyZacharias.net.

sometimes it will be up to the professor. Your professor's preferences for citation will range from the simple to the complex, and the amount of marks devoted to citation will range from relaxed to rigid. Improper citation can significantly drop your grade on a paper for more rigid professors. If you fail to cite something at all when you use someone else's ideas, this is plagiarism, and you may be ejected from the course or even from your degree program.

My (Ben's) first graduate teaching assignment consisted of teaching a class that was supposed to prepare students for seminary by teaching research, writing, and Turabian. There I was, in my first class, with eager, excited, and anxious seminarians ready to pursue their calling in ministry—to know him, show him, and share him—and I got to teach about commas.

In addition to exciting lectures on where commas go and the many other options for their usage, I had lectures on proper ordering of footnotes and bibliographies. Believe me—it is as boring as it sounds! But it is important. In order to convince questioning students of their importance, I played for them one of the famous speeches from

WHAT IS TURABIAN?

Kate L. Turabian (1893–1987) was the graduate school dissertation secretary at the University of Chicago from 1930 to 1958. During that time, she wrote a book that laid out the style students should adopt in their written work: *A Manual for Writers of Research Papers, Theses, and Dissertations*. This book became a standard style guide for academic work, and now it is often referred to simply as "Turabian." The style it describes is called "Turabian style" or "Chicago style."

the movie *Braveheart*. In this speech, Mel Gibson passionately, emotively, and compellingly convinces the armies of Scotland that the English could not take their freedom. Following this clip, I asked my students what made the message compelling. Was it the *words* of the message or the *way* he expressed his words (with the help of the direction and production team)? Following their discussion on this topic, I showed another video. In this second video the students heard *the exact same speech.* However, this time, the speech was made by a teenage girl in her basement with dim lights, a fake horse, and a homemade version of the classic *Braveheart* facepaint.

In these two examples, each speaker is using the same words and communicating the same message, but one is compelling and one is humorous. You may have a great message, you may understand theology or Greek or the nuances of church history, but if you cannot clearly communicate this message to your audience, then the lessons you have learned and the ideas you have clarified in life are *nearly* useless. Do not harm your message by failing to understand the requirements of how to communicate in a unique context. If, after seminary, you move overseas as a missionary, you will need to learn that language. You cannot expect the indigenous population to learn your southern drawl or your New York lingo. Instead, you are expected to learn *theirs!*

In the same way, at seminary you need to learn the language that is expected by the audience that will read and grade your papers. You get to learn Turabian, and commas, and active voice, and all of the other literary requisites for good writing at a graduate, theological institution.

For research essays, professors expect students to engage in the scholarly conversation that is already being carried out on their topic. A research paper should include quotations and references to academic research; these indicate the student's knowledge of the state of scholarship. Because engagement with sources is a primary component of research essays, citing sources properly is essential. When an author is quoted or an author's idea is used, it is the student's responsibility to cite accurately the source of the idea, concept, or quotation.

There are three basic ways sources are used within a research paper: as a reference, a quote, and a block quote. Of these three, references should be the most frequent. In most instances, a summary of what the secondary source says is sufficient and preferred, which means quotations should be used more sparingly. A direct quotation should be made when an idea is articulated particularly well, or when the essay will expound further on what the author has stated. A block quote is simply a quotation that takes up more than about five lines. In these cases, the quotation is not wrapped in quotation marks, but is instead single-spaced and indented.

Because the Bible is used so frequently in seminary and Bible college papers as a primary source, it does not usually require a full footnote. An in-text reference is usually sufficient. This means the biblical citation is included after the quotation, in parentheses, and before the period: "For all have sinned and fall short of the glory of God" (Rom 3:23 ESV). Besides the abbreviation of the biblical book and the chapter and verse, include the abbreviation of the version used. If you use the same version through your essay, note the version as above in the first quotation or in a footnote.

For ancient sources other than the Bible and Apocrypha, some style guides require the first quotation from a primary source to include a full bibliographic citation. Any subsequent quotations from the same body of literature would only need the in-text parenthetical citation. So, for example, when you quote from Josephus's *Antiquities of the Jews* it would look like this: "Those who undertake to write histories do not, I perceive, take that trouble on one and the same account, but for many reasons, and those such as are very different one from another" (Josephus, *Ant.* 1.1).[1] Any further quotations from Josephus using Whiston's translation would not need a footnote, just the in-text citation. Other style guides may want a footnote every time, but a shortened version after the first occurrence. Be sure that you know what is expected of you.

There are several styles of citation, and sometimes different styles are used by different professors in the same institution. Be sure to check your syllabus for what method of citation your professor wants, and if it isn't specified, ask directly. Both a writing tutor and your school's librarian can help you find the right sources for learning proper citation style. You may also be able to consult your school's writing guide. Your skill at citation can also greatly improve if you use the right tools (see chapter 10).

CONCLUSION

Like any skill, research takes practice. The more time you invest in developing your research skills, the better your papers will become. Good research skills can make the difference between a C paper and an A paper. Researching can be time consuming, but learning how to find quality sources for your research sets you up for success and

---

1. William Whiston, ed., *The Works of Josephus: Complete and Unabridged* (Peabody: Hendrickson, 1987).

will open up whole worlds of knowledge to you. As this chapter has introduced different types of academic literature, how to find good sources, and how to cite them, the next chapter will tackle the topic of how to actually read what you find.

CHAPTER 9

Reading and Writing Skills

For some seminary students, writing papers is the most challenging and frightening prospect of seminary. Students who received a bachelor of arts are often fairly comfortable writing papers, but others are coming out of a science or trades degree, or may have been out of school for many years. You may feel overwhelmed when it comes to paper writing because you have never been taught how to write an academic paper, or you may lack confidence in your writing ability in general.

You are going to spend a lot of your time reading and writing in seminary. And if you are intent on growing after seminary, both will continue to be a regular habit and discipline in your life. Because reading and writing occupy a significant amount of your time, you should be methodical and systematic in your approach to both. In my (Danny's) first year of post-secondary education at a one-year Bible school, I made the mistake of diving into books the same way I always had. This gave me the same results I always had: I forgot what I read, had no notes, and often had to re-read. In seminary, you can't afford to waste your time. You need to get the most you can out of your reading.

The same goes for writing. Simply writing more doesn't always yield better results, but deliberate practice will help your writing improve. If writing is a persistent struggle for you, we suggest that you either book regular sessions with your university's writing center or invest in a writing tutor.

You should also seek to learn from good writing as you read. There are certain strategies that are common to all great writers, and there are numerous examples of great writing in the library (and also poor writing, which will teach you what *not* to do). As you read, listen to the author's tone and observe the style. If you like it, try to mimic it. If you know a few people whose writing you admire, you can also ask them outright what strategies they use. What follows are some specific guidelines for how to improve your reading and writing skills.

DIFFERENT KINDS OF READING

In seminary, you will need to read differently than you do when you read for fun. Some of you already might have learned this in your undergraduate studies, but others of you may find it odd to think that there are different kinds of reading. When you are studying, you should *not* be reading the same way you just finished reading your last engrossing novel. You read a novel curled up on your sofa with a blanket and a warm drink. You read it from beginning to end. You are reading for the sheer delight and entertainment of it.

While you (hopefully) will enjoy learning, reading for learning is different from reading for entertainment.

It is an active exercise aimed at information extraction. I (Danny) had a teacher once who called all of his books his friends that he had conversations with. This analogy has stuck with me. I encourage students to think of their textbook and essay authors as teachers, because after all, they will be teaching you something. And there are a few things about these textual teachers that are *even better* than live teachers:

- They (usually) stay on topic.
- They don't let others interrupt their train of thought.
- You can rewind and fast-forward their discussion. You can pause them, go back to listen one more time to what they said, and even check out the ending first.

As you open up one of these new teachers, come with the purpose of understanding their arguments and information—not for entertainment.

DECIDE IF IT IS WORTH READING

Because not everything you come across is worth reading, you need to be able to decide whether to spend time with it. For instance, your assigned textbooks should be read thoroughly in the order your professor suggests, because in choosing that textbook, they are telling you that they have chosen this book as a coteacher for the course.

Reading for an assignment is different though. In these cases you need to do some quick evaluation to decide whether you should read it, and if so, how deeply you should read it. Whether it is a book or an article, take time to know what it is about; otherwise you will end up wasting time reading it only to learn you shouldn't have bothered. If it is a journal article, many have an abstract (a summary of the contents) at the beginning. There are also databases that abstract articles for you; to gain access to these, search your library website or ask your librarian how to access *New Testament Abstracts, Old Testament Abstracts,* and *Religious and Theological Abstracts.* If it is a book, find an academic book review in *ATLAS* or search for one using Google Scholar (scholar.google.com). If you can't find an abstract or book review, then you need to do a superficial review by looking over the table of contents and reading the introduction and conclusion.

Once you have done this, it is time to decide if it is worth reading more. Keeping your topic in mind, decide if:

- It is not worth *any* more time, because it does not speak to your topic.
- It is worth *a little* more of your time, because it is somewhat related to your topic. Decide how much time, and spend this time seeking to understand the broad outline of what the author is trying to convince you of and the points that lead to the conclusion.
- It is worth a *full front-to-back read.* This is a major decision, because reading does take time, and you need to jealously guard your time. If something is right on topic, read the book well. But remember that when you are researching for a paper, there are very few full books that are worthy of a full front-to-back read.

TAKE NOTES, HIGHLIGHT, UNDERSTAND

If you've decided to read something, don't curl up on the couch! Sit up while you are reading, and have a pen and paper or your laptop nearby to take notes. You are reading for information, so your job is to extract that information. Here is a simple tip to increase your reading speed: Use a pen or your finger to go back and forth on the page.

That pointer forces you to stay at a good pace. Trust us, it works!

If you are not taking notes while reading, you are not doing it right. Notes are a mental system for jogging your memory to remember what you read. Longtime Dallas Theological Seminary professor Howard Hendricks captured the importance of note taking with the phrase, "A pen is a mental crowbar."

The processes and types of note taking vary from person to person. Some people like to scribble notes right inside their books (make sure you don't use this method on library books), while others use Post-It notes in their books. Some people prefer to think with a mind map on paper, or with mind-mapping software. For both class and reading, a popular method is the Cornell note-taking system.[1] We encourage you to experiment with different types of note-taking systems and offer a few software options for note taking in chapter 10.

Because most of my (Danny's) reading is done electronically within Logos Bible Software, I use the highlighting and note-taking options within Logos. I try to minimize the amount of times that I pause while reading—I highlight quickly and press forward. After each chapter, I write out a summary of the chapter and place it in my reference manager (mentioned in chapter 10). When I am completely done with the book, I review both my summaries, as well as all of my highlights, and make notes on highlighted portions as needed.

The process for a physical book is similar, except that instead of highlighting, I make a simple dot or bracket in the margin with a pencil. Thus, at the end of reading,

---

1. For a brief explanation of this system, see lsc.cornell.edu/wp-content/uploads/2015/10/Cornell-Note_Taking-System.pdf.

I conclude by typing out the relevant notes and quotations and then place them in my reference manager.

If this sounds like a lot of work, it is! This is part of our point. Because it is a lot of work, don't weigh yourself down with reading every word or going back and rereading the last paragraph for the third time. Instead, press on—you've got a lot of work ahead of you and you need to get going.

The purpose of taking notes is for you to understand what you are reading and be able to recall it later. In thirty seconds, you should be able to describe the purpose of what you just read. What are the main points, and what conclusion was drawn? For every article, essay, book chapter, and book you read, it may be helpful to write a paragraph summary of it for yourself. If you can do this, you are reading with understanding.

DON'T MULTITASK

Reading requires your attention. That may seem obvious, yet you will be tempted to try to simultaneously watch something on your laptop, listen to music, carry on a texting conversation with a friend, or watch over your children. This won't work well (and you know it). So don't fool yourself by saying you are multitasking.

READING FOR INFORMATION EXTRACTION

If you would like to learn more about my method of reading and note taking, I present it in greater detail in a video course on my website (dannyzacharias.net/reading-for-information-extraction).

Except for combining a very regular and mundane activity like walking while listening to a podcast, or eating and reading the newspaper, multitasking is a myth.[2] All you are actually doing is rapid task-switching. This results in less focus on the tasks at hand and reduces your attention span. Instead of interrupting yourself in the guise of multitasking, turn on some music, but make it instrumental. Turn off your messaging service. Turn off your email. And be somewhere where you won't be interrupted by friends. Devote your attention to what you are actually doing.

KNOW THE NATURE OF THE ASSIGNMENT

When it comes time to put your own thoughts on paper (and ideally before), keep in mind what it is you need to be writing. Sometimes it will be a personal reflection. Sometimes your professor wants you to interact with a single book. Other times it is a full-blown research paper in which you need to interact with multiple sources. Find out the specifics! As soon as you begin a class that has written assignments, be sure to understand thoroughly what the teacher is looking for, especially if the syllabus is not very specific. If an assignment is unclear on the syllabus and you wait until the week before it is due to ask for clarification, the fault lies with you. Ask your professor if your professor has an example you can see. You can also ask if they have a teaching assistant (TA) you can meet with over lunch to pick their brain.

When you are choosing a paper topic, check with your professor or the TA to be sure you are on the right track. Common feedback you will often receive is:

---

2. Christine Rosen, "The Myth of Multitasking," thenewatlantis. com/publications/the-myth-of-multitasking.

Your argument is too broad.

You are covering three topics in one. Pick one.

Your thesis statement or research question is unclear. I'm not quite sure what you are trying to say.

All of these things are helpful to know before you start writing to make sure you do not waste time going down a dead end in your research. Get feedback as soon as you can.

START ASSIGNMENTS EARLY

Once you know what the teacher is expecting, you need to start as soon as you can. Managing your time well is one of the keys to putting yourself on track for writing success (see chapter 5). Since professors provide a syllabus on the first day of class that lists all the assignments, you have months to plan in advance of the deadlines.

The benefits of starting early cannot be stressed enough. First, by avoiding cramming, you avoid the guilt and stress associated with it. That in itself is worth its weight in gold. If you value your health and mental well being, not to mention your academic record, you will start early.

Second, it takes time to be creative. If you don't think you have a creative mind, that may be because you haven't given yourself enough time to be creative. By planting your paper topic in your head, you've given your subconscious an opportunity to work on it—on the bus, visiting your parents' house, in the shower, eating dinner, doing the laundry, or just zoning out. When those ideas come to you, all you have to do is jot them down with a note-taking tool (see chapter 10).

Third, getting an early start will give you an opportunity to take advantage of the writing help that is available to you. Have your first few papers done well in advance so that you can take it to the writing center or go over it with a tutor. If you have peers who are willing to proofread, this gives them time to do that.

Fourth, starting early will also give you time to proofread your own work. Proofreading your own writing is not particularly effective when it is done immediately after you have finished. You need time to distance yourself from when it was written. That way, the material is not as fresh in your mind and you come to your paper a little more impartially. Trust us; if you do this you will, at times, wonder what you meant! Refine. Refine. Then refine some more.

When proofreading, it also helps to change your environment. Danny learned this during the final phase of his PhD. He had a deadline to send the completed draft of his dissertation to his advisor. He had been pouring almost all of his time into this dissertation. In the last days, he was reading it over and over, editing, adding, and refining. It was two days away from the due date and he felt that he was done and ready to hit send. At the last second, he decided to do one more full read-through. Around that time, he had heard about the value of changing your surroundings for creativity. So somewhat reluctantly, he printed his entire disseration, grabbed a coffee, and moved to a different room at his college. As he read, he found many grammar and spelling mistakes, as well as dozens of sentences that needed to be more clearly written. He was quite shocked, as this material had passed before his eyes numerous times, and been read and edited by two separate advisors. But the different atmosphere and different medium (paper and pen rather than keyboard and screen) helped him see things he had missed earlier.

Giving yourself time means you have plenty of opportunity to rework, restructure, and revise. Not to mention that you can afford to forgo writing on those days when you lack the will. Remember that good writing takes time, so make every effort to give yourself that time.

ENGAGE WITH YOUR SOURCES

Often the most daunting and misunderstood tasks of paper writing in higher education is the need to interact with your sources, so we want to be sure that you understand clearly what your professors want. In a word, they want you to *engage*.

When writing research papers, you are expected to enter into the conversation of the topic at hand. This is difficult because you will *almost always* be speaking from a position of less knowledge than the authors you read. We understand that you would feel more comfortable summarizing the arguments and discussion that you read—but summarizing is only a portion of a research paper. You are also expected to enter into the conversation. You need to critique what you read, agreeing with some authors and not others. This engagement needs to be done while you build your own argument based on the research you do. So your own argument will be at times based on points which some authors make, and at times in opposition to what some authors say. Whether you agree or disagree, you need to be able to articulate why.

It is also not uncommon to come across a book or journal article with which you entirely agree. It will be tempting to overly use this source instead of continuing your research pursuits. Even in these instances where you find yourself agreeing entirely with an author, you need to construct an argument in your own words and use that author as support for your own argument.

MAINTAIN PROPER STYLE

Writing research papers is not like other kinds of writing. Research papers require a particular style, and the sooner you learn to write using this style the better. Here are a few tips for helping you maintain proper paper-writing style.

Unless the paper is meant to be a personal reflection, avoid using the first person (*I* or *we*) if possible. The exception is when you are drawing conclusions that are your own. Related to this, avoid colloquial language. For example, state that "the Gospel of Mark is a fast-paced narrative" rather than "Jesus seems to be zooming around in Mark."

Avoid rhetorical questions and questions that you immediately answer. Instead, make statements.

Have a clear introduction and conclusion. The introduction should state what you are intending to say, and the conclusion should recap what you have said. Nothing new should be stated in your conclusion.

Eliminate wordiness in your writing. Be clear and succinct in your statements so that the reader understands what you are saying, rather than getting confused by how it is stated. Use a thesaurus to discover words that convey the precise meaning of a concept or idea.

Prefer the active voice. It is stronger and more direct than the passive voice. An example of a passive sentence is: "The dog was seen by the boy." The active form is: "The boy saw the dog."

To emphasize text, use italics or bold, not quotation marks. But use even these sparingly.

Avoid both run-on sentences and sentence fragments. The grammar check built into Microsoft Word should catch many instances of this, but not all. You should always run both the grammar and spell-check before completing your paper. If you are not using Word, Google Docs also has a grammar and spell-check. You can also use grammar tools such as Grammarly.com or Ginger (a Google Chrome extension).

Avoid the use of superlatives or absolutes, such as "most," "all," "best," and so on. In most cases, these are statements of opinion that cannot be verified. Avoid weak adverbs, such as "very," and avoid overused words, such as "like."

Pay close attention to subject-verb and verb tense consistency. That is, singular subjects take singular verbs and plural subjects take plural verbs; the same verb tense (past, past perfect, present, and so on) should be used consistently throughout a paragraph. Grammar, spelling, punctuation, formatting, clarity—all of these things matter, so don't be sloppy.

FORMATTING YOUR PAPER

The formatting and style guide for your seminary will usually specify the format of your title page and particulars on how to number the pages. These are usually available online; ask if you don't know where to find it. Place the page number in the bottom center of each page unless your professor has specified otherwise, and follow guidelines on whether your title page is numbered or not. According to some style guides, the very first paragraph after a subheading should not be indented. This is a relatively minor issue, but the important point is to be consistent throughout your paper.

Notice that we have used headings and subheadings throughout this book. These make the reading experience more pleasant by helping a reader to see a flow in what you write. If you use the default heading styles in Microsoft Word or another word processor, some of the formatting of subheadings will already be done for you. For example, there will be an extra line between the previous section and the new subheading. The primary heading will be capitalized and bold. Headings should always occur on the same page as the first two lines of the following paragraph—in other words, don't have a heading at the very bottom of the page and then begin the next paragraph at the top of the next page. Again, if you use default heading styles in your word processor, they will automatically prevent this from happening. Also try to avoid having only one paragraph under a heading.

Fonts should also be consistent, with the body of the text being twelve point and the footnotes ten or eleven point, unless otherwise indicated by your institution. The heading fonts should also be consistent. Finally, the body of the text should always be aligned to the left—which is usually the default in word processors.

SAMPLE STEPS FOR A PAPER ON JESUS AND DIVORCE

After reading the above advice, you may still be wondering where to begin. In this case, you may want to break your writing assignment into individual steps. Create a list of small items that need to be done for each paper and then work on them one at a time. Breaking up large assignments into smaller, more manageable segments is the best way to make a daunting task more manageable. Here is a sample list of tasks to accomplish when writing a ten-page paper on Jesus' teaching on divorce for a New Testament class.

1. Read the syllabus and any applicable material from the professor to properly understand what is required.

2. Seek any necessary clarification from the professor and ask for an example paper, if possible.

3. Talk briefly with the professor to make sure that your topic (Jesus' teaching on divorce) satisfies the professor. Take anything he or she says into consideration and adjust accordingly.

4. Read articles on divorce in Bible dictionaries. Make notes and identify key Bible passages.

5. Scan the bibliographies of these dictionary articles and list items that particularly speak to Jesus' teaching on divorce.

6. Using bestcommentaries.com, identify the top academic commentaries you should consult about the key passages you have identified.

7. In the commentaries you read, scan the bibliography and/or footnotes of the passage for additional sources not mentioned in the dictionary articles.

8. Now that you have a basic grasp of the issue from reading the articles and commentary sections, write a preliminary outline of your paper (a simple bulleted list will suffice). Each bullet point will serve as a subheading in your paper.

9. Decide if you need to reduce your list of sources. If your source list is too short, use *ATLAS* to find more.

10. Use *ATLAS* and your library's database to acquire your sources. If they are available to you online through your library subscription, download them. If they are not available through your library, make a request for them from the library. Plan a time to take a trip to the library to retrieve those that are on the shelves.

11. Using the tips from chapter 10, extract the information and take notes on the sources you've collected. Your notes need to stay organized so that they are useful for later. When taking notes and writing down ideas, keep your paper outline in mind so that you know where your notes and ideas belong within the flow of your paper.

12. Some people prefer to read everything and then write, while others prefer to read and write a bit at a time when they feel the need. Whichever way you choose, revise your paper outline as you research, and keep your notes organized.

13. Write the first draft of your introduction. State exactly what you are going to argue and the conclusion you will draw. This isn't a suspense novel; you don't need to surprise your professor in the conclusion. State in the introduction exactly what you are going to argue, argue it in the body, then restate what you just said in the conclusion.

14. Using your notes and sources, work on the content under your first subheading. As you go, do not forget to properly footnote your sources. Whenever you directly quote a source or directly refer to it and an argument it makes, footnote the source. (It is *much better* to cite properly as you are writing rather than leave it to the end.) Repeat this process for each subheading.

15. Write the first draft of your conclusion. Revise your introduction to be sure it matches your conclusion.

16. Spell-check. Grammar check. Proofread. Be sure your citation style conforms to your professor's request.

17. Insert page numbers and make sure the title page is how your professor wants it.
18. If you have followed our advice on time management and given yourself five to seven days to spare, put it aside for a few days.
19. If this is one of your first papers, arrange a session with your school's writing center or a writing tutor to go over the paper with you.
20. If you have chosen a friend to proofread for you, give it to them to proofread.
21. Do your own final proofread and edit.
22. Submit.

While this may seem like a long list, in reality many of these steps will only take minutes and some are done simultaneously. Bear in mind, too, that you will get better with practice. You will start flying through a lot of these steps, you won't always need to be accessing a writing tutor, and soon you will be so good at picking topics that you won't need to even check with your professor.

If you are still intimidated by the prospect of writing papers, remember that you are wired to want to finish the things you start. I (Danny) had the dream of this book in my mind long before it came to fruition. It wasn't until I sat down one day, opened my word processor, and typed the title that the first domino was pushed over, which eventually led to the last domino falling. So don't hem and haw over that major assignment, just START! Once you do, the positive mental pressure it exerts will spur you toward completion.

GET FEEDBACK FROM THE GRADER

Once the paper is turned in, your work is not done. If you want to become a better writer, you need to seek out feedback. Some professors are better than others at offering feedback on assignments, so be bold and ask. As we mentioned in chapter 4, stick a note on the front of the paper saying:

"Dear Dr. _____, I'd like to ask that you (or your TA) please offer me as much feedback as you can on every aspect of my paper. I want to learn from my mistakes, so please be critical and don't hold back. Thanks very much for your assistance."

After handing in your paper, book a time with your professor to go over what you did well and where you need improvement, particularly if you did not feel that you received adequate feedback. This feedback will be an invaluable source of information that you can take with you to your next writing project. If the teacher cannot meet with you, then ask if the TA can go over it with you. If that can't happen, then take your paper to your writing tutor or the writing center and go over all of the feedback you received.

You won't need to do this for every assignment, but do it as much as possible in your first semester or two. Soon, you will have come so far in your writing skills that you could be the tutor.

PRESENTATIONS

Sometimes rather than presenting your research in writing you will need to give a presentation in front of your classmates and professor. Many of the skills you use for communicating in writing will apply here as well. When it comes to presentations, though, make slides that are engaging, with nice photos and not too much text. Prepare some handouts for the class, and practice what you are going to say beforehand. Get feedback from a fellow classmate if possible.

Be the kind of presenter you would like to listen to: Don't just read a prepared statement with no eye contact and too many verbal fillers such as "um," "uh," and "like." (Side note: Don't use these three words during corporate prayer either!) Your aim is to engage and enlighten every person in the room with what you say and how you said it. If you have a classmate say "that was really good," or "thanks, I learned a lot," or "I enjoyed listening to you more than the professor!" then you know you've done well!

CONCLUSION

You may have been reading and writing since you were very young, but you are in a whole new world now. You'll come across words you've never seen before, and there will be times when you read a page over and over again because you just aren't understanding it. You'll also encounter times when you're just not sure how to get your thoughts to come out in the right way on paper.

POPULAR PRESENTATION TOOLS

- PowerPoint is Microsoft's presentation software. It is included with the Microsoft Office productivity suite (products.office.com/en-us/powerpoint).

- Keynote is Apple's presentation software. It can be purchased individually (apple.com/keynote).

- Prezi is a cloud-based presentation software. It uses a subscription model in which you pay for a year at a time (prezi.com).

- If you are on a tight budget, Google Docs is free and includes Google Slides (slides.google.com).

That's okay.

You are entering into a new field of study, and your professor and the writers you read all went through the same process. Like almost every new skill you've ever acquired, academic reading and writing are skills that you will develop over time. And like every new skill, you get better with practice, by not giving up, by *wanting* to get better, and by cutting yourself some slack during the learning process.

We both have read many (many) books, but there are still times, particularly when we are reading outside of our fields of expertise, when we need to slow down and even backtrack because we have lost the author's argument. When I (Danny) was an undergraduate student, I was a very poor writer. I soon realized that writing is a skill that is honed, not just something you're born with. Becoming a better writer is an ongoing process for everybody. Most of your professors still go through an editing and rewriting process for their academic publications. These uncomfortable times of growing in your reading and writing skills are like a mental gym. With grit and determination, the process will be a time of growth for you.

Finally, consider that learning how to read and write well will make a big difference in your life and career going forward. While most of you will not write any more academic papers after you graduate, paper writing is not a pointless exercise. Academic reading and writing are *highly transferable skills*. The process of putting together a good essay or exegesis paper forces you to read various views on a subject, engage in the conversation about the subject, and critique and articulate the arguments of others.

Even if you never write another paper, your overall communication skills will improve. You will gain skill in articulating your thoughts on a subject, learning from some arguments and rejecting others. You will be more comfortable engaging those with whom you disagree. You will be more confident in critiquing the arguments of others. In short, these skills teach you to think and articulate your thoughts well, which will help in whatever ministry or career you find yourself in.

CHAPTER 10

The Right Tools

There are numerous tools for your academic toolbelt that go hand in hand with the important skills we discussed in the previous two chapters. All of these tools, most of which are software applications, are designed to make a job easier for you. As with every tool, make sure that you learn how to use it effectively. It only takes a Google or YouTube search to find articles and video explanations on how to use these tools, so take the time not only to acquire the tools, but to learn how to use them.

I (Danny) remember sitting in a room at my seminary working on a paper. I was frustrated, and it showed. As I stared at my laptop, my Old Testament professor walked by and noticed the signs of distress. He asked if everything was all right, and I explained that I felt like I was spending as much time working on the proper formatting of my footnotes as I was the content of my paper. He then casually mentioned that there is now software that will properly do my footnotes and bibliography for me. After I picked my jaw up from the floor, I asked for the name of the app. I got it, and read the whole manual to figure it out. Before this, I was not savvy with technology, but that small investment in time made me realize the potential that software had to save me time. I then picked up the manual of my word processor and learned how to do all of the important things. After that, the potential for software to significantly aid in my research, studies, and productivity became very apparent to me. I became a tech convert.

In this chapter, we outline some of the productivity tools that we find helpful and think will be helpful to you. Many of you already have a system of productivity that works. If this is the case, practice what we said in the previous chapter about reading selectively and scan this chapter for new insights. Those of you who are less tech-savvy may want to give this chapter a closer reading.

Most of what is outlined below are digital tools, as this is the field that is constantly changing and adding new assistance to students in your shoes. The benefit of digital tools is that they are portable (you can carry them around on your laptop or smartphone) and you can install them on multiple devices. You can also keep your information synced between devices using cloud computing. Most of the following software applications are available on a variety of platforms: Mac and PC (for desktop and laptop computers), and iOS and Android (for smartphones and tablet computers).

CALENDAR/SCHEDULER

If you want to make sure you have time for the important stuff during your higher education years, then you need to be in control of your time. The particulars of how to schedule your semesters were dealt with in chapter 5, but one tool you need to accomplish this is a good calendar.

If you have a Mac, you already have an app called iCal built in. If you use a PC or Mac with Microsoft Office, you have Outlook. If you prefer an online version, Google Calendar is great. If you want something a little more specific to homework management, there are some good options too. A good Mac & iOS (for mobile devices) option is iStudiez Pro. One homework manager that crosses all platforms is the myHomework app. Finally, for those who still like traditional pen and paper, we suggest the academic version of the Passion Planner.

WORD PROCESSOR

We are often surprised at how many people don't know how to use their word processor (usually Microsoft Word)—even office workers who use it every day! You shouldn't have to wrestle at 3:00 a.m. with your word processor to get the page numbers right. Instead, be intentional and learn how to use it early on.

While Microsoft Word is the standard word processor, it can be overwhelming since it is made to do everything under the sun. However, one reason to choose Word is that it is used widely, so it is easy to exchange files with others

SCHEDULING TOOLS

- Google Calendar (google.com/calendar)
- iStudiez Pro (istudentpro.com)
- myHomework (myhomeworkapp.com)
- Passion Planner (passionplanner.com)

or open files on different computers. If you are a Mac user, Pages is Apple's alternative, though there is a version of Word for Mac as well. If you want something for free, OpenOffice or LibreOffice will do everything you need for writing papers. Google Docs is another free online option that can do pretty much everything you need it to as well. Mac users can also opt for Nisus Writer or Mellel, which is Danny's academic word processor of choice.

Whatever word processor you decide on (there are many others), be sure you know how to do at least these things:

1. Edit headers and footers
2. Create columns
3. Alter font size and line spacing
4. Add a footnote or endnote
5. Number pages (including how to use section breaks for restarting page numbers)
6. Check spelling (You have *zero* excuse for spelling mistakes with the technology you have access to!)

If you are involved in more advanced studies where you are writing larger pieces of work (like a thesis), then you also should become familiar with paragraph and heading styles—how to alter them and use them effectively. This will save you a lot of time. To learn how to do all these things, you can use the help files that are included in most programs. There are also usually video tutorials on You-Tube when you need more help.

NOTE-TAKING SYSTEM

We set out Danny's process for note taking in chapter 9. In terms of organization, it is a *very* good idea to keep all of your notes in the same place, or at least have a logical system for where notes will be. We also recommend going electronic with your notes, as the usefulness of your notes in the long term is largely based on their accessibility. For this reason we find electronic notes to be much more handy. They can be searched, added to, copied, and pasted.

The potential downside of electronic note taking is that some research indicates we learn better when taking notes by hand, as it involves the fine motor skills in the learning process.[1] Some people have combined the best of both worlds; they take notes by hand and then type them out digitally at a later time as a means of both review and storage. As technology changes and handwriting with tablet computers improves, the combination of handwriting and electronic storage may continue to improve. Experiment and find what works best for you.

The great thing about today's note-taking systems is that they are so much more than just a note taker—they are databases for you to store whatever you want. These programs make it easy for you to capture web pages, store Portable Document Formats (PDFs), and so on. They are digital filing cabinets that help you organize your thoughts without taking up a lot of space.

There are many digital options to choose from. If you have Microsoft Office, you may already have Microsoft OneNote installed. For Mac users, DEVONthink is a powerful database. The most popular note-taking and database system right now is Evernote. Evernote is available on all operating systems, including mobile, and is free up to a certain amount of storage and devices. Whatever

---

1. One article that discusses the benefits of taking notes by hand is Gwendolyn Bounds, "How Handwriting Trains the Brain," *Wall Street Journal* (October 5, 2010): wsj.com/articles/SB10001424052748 704631504575531932754922518.

you choose, become a guru for that software. Watch video tutorials and access the help files to learn how to make the best use of your database.

There are still other options for taking notes. Some programs, for example, will allow you to sync a live audio lecture with your notes. OneNote on a laptop can record audio while you take notes. Another option on the iPad is the app Notability, which does the same thing. If you want to combine writing by hand with digital notes and audio, you can purchase a LiveScribe SmartPen; it syncs your handwritten notes with live audio, and then digitizes your handwritten notes and sends them to your computer. (Wow!)

FLASH CARDS

Using good old flash cards is still one of the best ways to memorize large amounts of information. Fortunately for you, flash cards have also gone digital, so you don't need to carry around wads of cards anymore; you can access them on your computer or mobile device.

What's more, many times you won't even need to make the cards! Quizlet.com is a fantastic and free online resource for the exchanging of flash cards. Odds are that

NOTE-TAKING TOOLS

- Evernote (evernote.com)
- OneNote (onenote.com)
- DEVONthink (devontechnologies.com/products/devonthink)

the textbook you'll be quizzed on already has a set of flash cards that someone else has made, or that the publisher has made, that you can use. Quizlet can be used online and on mobile devices. Brainscape.com and Cerego.com are also popular online flash card web apps.[2]

CITATION SOFTWARE/REFERENCE MANAGER

We listed learning how to cite sources properly as an important skill in chapter 9. There are, thankfully, numerous tools to help you cite properly and manage your source information. We were still in college at the advent of reference managers and citation tools. Before finding this software, we would spend just as much time on our footnotes and bibliography as the research and writing! Working to properly format footnotes and bibliographies is painful. But when someone introduced us to software tools that could properly format our footnotes and bibliography, we immediately became adept at reference management software. You should too.

The most basic citation software is built into the latest versions of Microsoft Word (if you don't know where to find it, search the Help menu for "citations.") A more advanced option that still works within Word on PCs is EazyPaper. This program, which is available for purchase, will ask you to insert the information for a book or article, and it will properly format your footnotes and bibliography (as we mentioned in chapter 8, *be sure* to find out what citation style your professor or school wants).

If you are only writing a few papers, using Word citation styles or EazyPaper will serve you well. However, if you are specializing in an area in which you will be writ-

---

2. These and other varieties of flash card software are listed here: en.wikipedia.org/wiki/List_of_flashcard_software.

ing a lot of papers, or especially if you are heading to doctoral studies, you owe it to yourself to start using a more powerful reference management software. As professors and academics, our reference manager is one of the top tools in our toolbox. Not only will it save you hours by formatting your citations and bibliography correctly, but it will also be a place where you can store your articles and reading notes in a searchable database.

There are numerous options. The most well-known reference manager, available on both Mac and PC, is Endnote—but it is also the most pricey. An affordable Mac option is Bookends. For students on a budget, there are some popular and very good free options too. Zotero (cross platform), Mendeley (cross platform), Qiqqa (PC), and Sente (Mac, and Danny's tool of choice) are free for small databases. All sync to the cloud so you'll never lose your information, plus you can highlight and mark up PDFs directly in the software. Many reference managers are also scalable. While the basic version is free, you can pay for an increased amount of storage.

REFERENCE-MANAGEMENT TOOLS

- Endnote (endnote.com)
- Bookends (sonnysoftware.com)
- Zotero (zotero.org)
- Mendeley (mendeley.com)
- Qiqqa (qiqqa.com)
- Sente (thirdstreetsoftware.com)

BIBLE SOFTWARE

We are so blessed today with an unprecedented ability to study and access God's Word. While there are many free online tools for Bible study, in our opinion a more powerful Bible software application, like Logos, Accordance, BibleWorks, or WORDSearch, is one of the most important tools seminary students can place in their toolkit and for their ministry in the future. Bible software allows you to search the Bible and access top-quality resources with just a few clicks. Research that used to take hours and even days can now often be done with a few keystrokes. Several Bible software applications are available on PC, Mac, and mobile devices, and sync your highlights and notes across your devices.

Although we recognize that many people prefer physical books, Danny often recommends to his students that at a minimum they purchase reference works in their Bible software of choice. Reference works are defined as anything you wouldn't normally read straight through: Bible dictionaries, lexicons, commentaries, atlases, and so on. These resources become so much more powerful and useful when you can fully search them and open them up alongside your Bible. Danny has been recommending this practice to his students for many years, and not once has

BIBLE SOFTWARE TOOLS

- Logos (logos.com)
- Accordance (accordancebible.com)
- BibleWorks (bibleworks.com)
- WORDSearch (wordsearchbible.com)

any student expressed regret over using Bible software and building up their electronic library. In fact, he has had many students tell him that one of the most important things he taught them is how to use Logos Bible Software.

CONCLUSION

Unless you came of age in the years before the internet, odds are you are fairly comfortable with technology, particularly social aspects of the internet. But now is the time to tap into the power of the digital revolution and learn how to use tools that will help you thrive in seminary. There are many software options that can become valuable tools to save you time and effort so that you can focus on your studies. Find the right tools for your ministry toolkit and learn to use them effectively to maximize your time and efficiency in seminary.

Final Thoughts

—————— 🖋 ——————

Seminary education is a challenging and rewarding process, and we believe it is important to enter into your degree program with a plan and with your eyes wide open to all of the realities. This will enable students to get the most out of their time in seminary, to not be surprised by the demands and requirements placed upon them, and hopefully equip you to not succumb to the stressors and temptations that are too frequent in seminary student life. One of the keys for making it to the successful conclusion of graduation is to *remember*—especially in the midst of all the challenges, stresses, lessons, and joys that will most certainly face over the next few years.

In the pages of the Old Testament, God frequently reminded the Israelites to remember: their former enslavement the covenant they made, how he brought them out of Egypt. God knows we have bad memories. If you have had times of spiritual struggle or doubt, especially during seminary, these are the points when you need to stop and remember—in the midst of a stressful semester, after getting a bad grade, or sitting through a class with a dull professor. It is at these moments that remembering is most important, because it is here that you may wonder why you are putting yourself through the hardship that is seminary. You need to remember. Remember how God saved you, how you felt the strong presence of the Almighty, when you saw his hand powerfully working in your life. Remember the people and circumstances that brought you here in the first place. Remember the call that God has placed on your life. During times of stress or doubt, let these memories draw you back to your purpose and the reasons that you want to endeavor. We are able to persevere and get back on track through more difficult times when our foundations are secure.

You also want to *look forward*. The desire to get to the end goal is a good one, but when you finally walk across the stage to receive your degree, you don't want to do so with regrets. As you look forward, think about how you want to finish: knowing you did your best, that you worked hard, that you learned from mistakes, and that you are the better for it. By both looking back and looking forward you will be able to keep things in perspective, stay motivated, and be able to push through times of stress and setback.

Both of us want to thank you for joining us in this journey and making it to the end! Thank you for taking your seminary education seriously by preparing for it, and thank you for answering the call to ministry. Not only do we want you to survive and thrive in seminary, but we want you to use the foundation of your seminary experience to survive and thrive in ministry, for the glory and kingdom of our Lord and Savior.

Soli Deo Gloria,
H. Daniel Zacharias
Benjamin K. Forrest

——— 🖋 ———

Choosing a Seminary

While this book is primarily for students who are already in seminary or have already enrolled, we recognize that some readers may still be choosing a seminary. We recommend that readers in this situation clarify their thoughts in three areas.

First, think about how your personal doctrinal convictions line up with the school's theological positions. It is not likely you will find a one-to-one compatibility with any seminary, and it is possible that your convictions on some issues will change or become more nuanced as you study. But broadly speaking, if you are a Wesleyan, you *may* not want to choose a Presbyterian seminary.

The second is related to the direction of your calling. Does this school help you to accomplish the goals you have for your future ministry? If your goal includes pastoral leadership, then ask whether your denomination ordains or licenses graduates from this school. If your long-term plan is to move on to doctoral work or pursue higher education, ask about the numbers of graduates who are accepted into doctoral programs. Especially if your plan involves further education, give preference to those seminaries that are accredited. Essentially, accreditation means that a seminary has proven to its peers (other accredited seminaries) that it does its job with excellence, meets the goals of the school's mission statement, and offers an education that accomplishes the goals of the degree.

Third is the issue of cost, affordability, and stewardship. This is weighed in contrast and connection to the previous two issues, meaning that if your goals are the pastorate, then perhaps a school that is less expensive might be a wise decision. Likewise, if your goals are the professorate, know that the most prestigious schools are often the most expensive schools. Is the cost worth the leg up when it comes time to apply for a PhD program? In some cases the answer is yes, and in other cases it is probably no.

Other questions you could ask might include:

- Do I want to stay close to home to take advantage of free/cheap rent, or do I want to include the experience of moving (perhaps to the other side of the country or even another country) and becoming more independent?
- Is there a particular seminary that my pastors or spiritual mentors would recommend for me?
- What is my financial *reality* (emphasis on *reality* instead of hypothesized reality)? Do I have the financial freedom to choose any seminary I want, or do I need to confine myself to one of the cheaper options?

- Is my spouse on board? Are there any parameters or restrictions he/she would make? What would be best for my children? Is there a school where we have family nearby who might provide support?
- Should I consider a fully online degree or a fully residential degree? Should I pursue the degree full time or part time? Should I work during seminary, or should we, as a family, plan for my spouse to work?

There is no one-size-fits-all answer to these questions. As you answer them, take into account your own learning style as well as areas where you need to grow. Honestly assess your strengths and weaknesses. If you sense a need to grow in independence, a move across the country may be exactly what you need at this stage of life. If you have already been in pastoral ministry and know that your preaching is weak, consider finding a school that specializes in training preachers. Alternatively, you may identify strengths that you can turn in to super strengths (by choosing a school that specializes in this area).

In your consideration of an online or residential program, you should also carefully consider your personality traits and learning style. Someone who feels a strong call to pastoral ministry but who is also shy or introverted may benefit greatly from a residential setting where they are sitting with people face to face in a classroom. Some extroverts may also receive a better education from a residential program because they derive their energy and excitement from being around others, making a fully online program a difficult task. In other cases, you may already be a pastor or lay-leader in your church, and instead of choosing to pass this role on to another shepherd, you instead might wisely and necessarily choose an online program. Or, you might be the sole provider for your family and giving up a consistent paycheck may not be a realistic option. In this case, or similar cases, an online degree or a blended program might meet your academic goals while allowing you to remain where you are.

Whatever the case, we recommend that you go into the decision with your eyes wide open. There is no perfect school or situation, so we encourage you to think through the challenges and opportunities that will come from your decision to attend seminary. Our advice is to work to limit the challenges and harness the opportunities.

Paying for Seminary

Debt is one of the greatest stressors for students. Watching the hole get deeper every year you are in school makes you feel out of control and anxious. If you multiply the total tuition for a year at your seminary (or the seminaries that you are considering) by three (typically an MDiv takes at least three years), you will get the minimal cost of your degree. Now add this number to the total amount of debt you have remaining from your undergraduate education and ask: Do I want to have this much debt hanging around my future ministry plans? If not, consider carefully the advice that follows, which is born from our own experiences and decisions (both good and bad).

We are going to be up front with you: We failed miserably at the financial aspects of seminary! We are not, even now, free from our education debt. One reason for this was lack of education. I (Danny) didn't grow up in a home that taught about money; my parents lived paycheck to paycheck and spent their money poorly. I also assumed along with most students that in order to go to school, I had to take out student loans. I prized this temporary freedom because it allowed me to focus on school and not worry about juggling a part-time job. I went through almost my entire secondary education before I wised up. I could have buckled down through my education, worked a part-time job, and minimized my debt.

Unwise choices regarding student loans might seem simple and innocent at the time, but when compounded over the years, they create a mountain of debt that can take several years to climb. We have reaped the "blessings" of student loans—meaning we are still paying them! Our choice to rely on debt to pay for school has affected our entire family, and trying to help you is part of our penance. In this appendix, we will give you some advice about how to pay for seminary—advice we wish we'd had before we enrolled.

COMMIT TO MINIMIZING DEBT

Even if you have decided that some level of debt is unavoidable, you must commit to having as little debt as possible. This is hard to do; the consequences of student debt don't always hit home until student loan or credit card statements arrive at your door or in your email inbox. Only then are you required to face the true cost of the decisions you made during academic study. Here are just a few additional costs you incur while paying off your debt:

- Potential savings and giving instead go toward loan repayment.
- There is potential to get further into debt in order to live while repaying student debt.

- It may be hard to find additional money to save for your first home or car.
- You will be paying your landlord's mortgage through rent payments instead of building equity for yourself through a mortgage.
- Your credit rating will suffer if your payments aren't on time.
- Payments will drain your financial resources, specifically money for fun stuff.
- You are unable to accept a ministry position you really want or need for career experience, because they don't pay enough to cover your debt repayment and living expenses.

This last point often can be significant. Quite often, seminary graduates come out of their education with significant debt that they have no choice but to tackle almost immediately. Part of this pressure can mean that students will take the first church that calls them. The pressure of debt may cause you to accept the call to a church not because God is leading you, but because you need the money. If you minimize debt, you will keep it from having influence over your decisions.

Some of you may already have debt from your undergraduate education. If that is the case, you need to commit to not adding any more to your debt load, or choose to pay off your undergraduate debt before moving into graduate studies. While ministry can be one of the most rewarding jobs on the planet, it certainly is not the best paying career. This can be a difficult decision for you; you want to get into your education and get on to ministry! But taking on too much debt is not worth it.

One of the best ways to minimize student debt is to pay for courses as you can afford them. Many students overlook this option because it will take you longer to complete your studies. You may have relocated your spouse or family and there is pressure to finish swiftly. You may believe you are losing out on income—the money you would have earned had you completed your studies sooner. Typically you also receive more scholarships if you are studying full time. Truth be told, seminaries would prefer that you study full time. But if you are studying full time and not earning any income, you are going to be enslaved to debt later.

Don't fool yourself into believing you'll get some high-paying job in the summer either. This usually does not happen. Instead, have the money in the bank for your classes, or be certain that you can make regular payments during the semester so that you can pay for each semester as it comes to a close. In a few years, you can graduate and charge out into ministry with no or minimal debt—an amount you can pay off in a year or two. Or else, along with most of your peers, you will be drowning in debt for many years to come.

START A BUDGET AND CUT DOWN ON UNNECESSARY EXPENSES

Overspending happens easily when you are not taking charge of your finances. Your resources are meant to serve you, not the other way around. The best way to take charge of your finances is to budget. As Dave Ramsey teaches, tell every dollar where to go.[1] There are plenty of budgeting software options; I (Danny) use YNAB, which stands for "You Need a Budget." If you are already in debt, start working to get rid of it. If you need a crash course in

---

1. "A Zero-Based Budget: Where and Why," daveramsey.com/blog/zero-based-budget-what-why.

money management, find a church that offers Dave Ramsey's Financial Peace University or has Good $ense materials in their lending library. Go through them (with your spouse if married) and begin to apply the principles, even if they seem drastic!

No single extravagant expense cripples the financial life of a student more than a car. Parking, gas, maintenance, and insurance all add up for someone on a tight budget. Unless there is no way to commute or take public transit, we recommend you avoid a car at all costs. Even if someone is willing to buy you a car while you are studying, the monthly expenses for gas and upkeep may not be worth it. Instead, you can live closer to school, find a job closer to school (this will save you from having to work to pay for your car), or take public transportation.

If you still feel you need a car, get yourself an old beater on a classifieds site like Craigslist or an equivalent site in your area. If you or your spouse are not handy, find someone in your church who will help you maintain your rust bucket during your studies.

Another unnecessary expense to look out for is new technology. Although it is nice to have the latest and greatest technology, think carefully before diving in. Is buying a laptop a good investment in your education? Absolutely. Is a smartphone? It depends. The service fees alone

BUDGETING TOOLS

- YNAB (youneedabudget.com)
- EveryDollar (everydollar.com)
- Mint (mint.com)

may add to your student debt quickly and it is difficult to get out of a contract once you commit, particularly if you want the latest and greatest instead of settling for the free model. When deliberating, ask yourself which is most important: reducing your debt or having the convenience of technology you want but can live without. If you really feel you need a cell phone just for safety, there are cheaper options than the latest smartphone. Remember, too, that many campuses offer wireless internet, and you can use apps like MagicJack, Ooma, or Google Voice to call any North American number for free over WiFi. And you can use a free texting app for text messaging.

Another thing you really need to say no to is eating out. We know it is fun to go out for wing night or hit the local burger shack for a late night snack with your peers. But choosing to eat out when you can't afford it is choosing a debt lifestyle. The truth is, not only is eating at home cheaper, but if you go and buy the groceries with that same group of friends and cook and enjoy the meal together, it will be even more fun. Call us old fashioned, but we still think relationships grow the fastest in the kitchen and around the dinner table at home.

During the day, you should be packing your lunch. Colleges/universities and local restaurants make a fortune selling you food, coffee, pastries, and just about everything else. You'll save yourself a pile of money if you pack your lunch and bring a thermos of your own favorite coffee or tea—that daily Starbucks run could pay for a whole course!

Finally, minimize your travel expenses. For students who have moved some distance to attend seminary, study week (if your institution has these) and Christmas break are times to hop a plane and head back home. But if you are on a strict budget and keeping debt at bay, then you need to resist the urge to go home so often. If someone is willing to pay for your trip, then by all means go for it. But how much better will your semester be if you actually use study week to study? And how much better will your financial situation be later?

If you do all these things, your friends will think you are frugal. Guess what? They're right. You will also be the one saving hundreds of dollars every month, and you won't be crawling out of debt for years after graduating like everyone else! I (Danny) have a good friend from seminary whose wife kept the budget—and boy was she frugal. He had a very low monthly budget she gave him to spend on coffee, chips, etc. He would often refrain from going out with us to the local coffee shop because he had used up his small allowance for the month. At the time I wondered how anyone could live like that. But they graduated with very little debt, and I'll be paying my debt off for years.

BE SMART ABOUT YOUR HOUSING

You need to find the cheapest accommodations possible, even if they aren't that pretty. If you are single, find a single room with shared facilities. And if you are married and possibly with children, think together: would we rather stick it out in an ugly but cheap spot during seminary, or live in comfort during this time and struggle under our debt load later? I (Danny) was fortunate to live in a small town with no unsavory neighborhoods to speak of. In your situation, you have to take safety into consideration and make use of your collective parental radar. The less money you can spend on housing, the more money you have to pay for tuition, thereby limiting debt. Otherwise you will have increased debt that will limit your living choices *after* graduation; the not-so-pretty accommodations after seminary may last a lot longer as you reap the consequences of your earlier decision.

You should also rent month-to-month if possible. During the summer, many students choose to move elsewhere in order to earn money for next year's tuition. Unfortunately, if you have signed a year-long lease, you're stuck paying for an apartment or perhaps trying to find a subletter for the remaining months. If you cannot find a subletter, you will spend a good chunk of your summer earnings on rent that could have been saved for next year.

If the landlord really wants a year-long agreement, see if you can negotiate a slightly higher monthly payment for an eight- or nine-month contract. Also let your landlord know that you are a seminary student and more mature than younger students might be. Often rent has a built in fix-everything-after-the-crazy-college-kids-move-out fund. If you let your landlord know you aren't one of those students, they may just reduce the rent.

SEEK OUT ALTERNATIVE FORMS OF FUNDING
Whatever your financial position, it is always wise to look for creative ways to pay for seminary. The first thing to do is look into scholarships and bursaries on the financial aid website of your college or university. This is one of the major sources of revenue students often overlook as part of their financial planning for diploma or degree studies. There can be several varieties of financial aid:

- *Entrance scholarships.* These are based on academic merit. The higher your grades upon entrance, the more money you will receive. Many students are considered for scholarships automatically when they apply, while other scholarships require that you submit an application.

- *In-course scholarships.* These are scholarships students can receive as they progress through their academic program. Again, the higher the grades you achieve, the more money you will receive. Most in-course scholarships are awarded automatically.
- *Transfer scholarships.* These are available to students coming from another institution. If the institution you intend to apply to offers transfer scholarships, then it is certainly worthwhile to submit an application if one is required.
- *Bursaries (or grants).* Bursaries are based on financial need and are like scholarships in that they do not need to be repaid. Keep in mind that students who have submitted and qualify for government financial assistance are more likely to qualify for bursaries since the two are often linked.

Sometimes you can ask family members for financial assistance. If this is the case, do so humbly and be sure to let them know you completely understand if they cannot help you. But remember, if you follow all of these tips, then even twenty dollars a month from several family members will help you. Depending on your seminary, your family members may be able to pay it directly to the institution. When asking family for help, you should also be sure that you pledge to pay it forward. Tell them that you promise to do the same thing for other family members in the future.

You can also ask your church (both your home church and the church you attend while in seminary) for help. If you are doing ministry in a church that cannot afford to pay you, ask the leadership team to consider putting a salary for you into the budget anyway. Or if you are being paid too little, ask them to increase the amount. Often churches do not have because they have not asked

God (Jas 4:2). Ask them to make a line in their budget on faith to pay you, and make it clear that this is the bottom priority of the budget (that is, money goes to it last). The worst that can happen is that the money doesn't come in, but God often responds to our faith steps!

There are frequently times during the year when an extra offering is taken—either a second offering during a service or a fifth Sunday in a month. Churches often use these offerings to go to something other than the operating budget. Ask that each year one of these special offerings go toward your seminary education. Ask that it be announced and put in the bulletin at least a month ahead of time.

Ask your church leadership to consider putting into place an education/training fund and have an informal understanding that you will be the designee of the fund during your education. Be sure to have the church designate the fund generally as an education fund—*not* as a fund specifically for you. This would be a fund that anyone could give to through the church. If the church agrees to this, let your family know that your church has put this in place. That way both your physical and church family can support your education and still receive a tax receipt.[2] This will encourage your church to be involved in supporting your education, and will encourage them to keep the fund going for others once you have finished your education. Also make sure to have this education fund printed as a regular line item in your weekly bulletin.

---

2. Since tax laws vary from place to place, we want to make clear that we are not accountants and what we're saying is no substitute for professional tax or legal advice. Before you try to put a fund like this in place, you should consult with an accountant or lawyer who is familiar with the tax laws where you live.

Find opportunities for pulpit supply. You may be able to repolish an Introduction to Homiletics sermon and present it again, or you can get practice writing original sermons. If you are in seminary, you are training for ministry. It is a good idea to proclaim the message you are studying to churches that are hungry for God's Word, so practice proclaiming (and get paid for it)!

If you have moved for your studies, talk with the leadership of your home church as well. Ask them to keep you in your prayers and see if they would consider some financial support for your education, be it an annual gift or perhaps a monthly contribution. Whatever the support may be, ensure that you take time during your years in seminary to keep in contact with your home church. Perhaps it is a Christmas letter, or maybe a short presentation when you are back home for the summer.

WORK LIKE A CRAZY PERSON

If you can handle it alongside your required ministry work, get a part-time job. (You have an undergraduate degree in *something*—put it to use!) When I (Ben) started seminary, the first day I was in town I interviewed to be a substitute teacher. I didn't get hired after that interview, and so I moved on and found a job as a waiter at a local Italian restaurant. There were at least three additional school districts within a short driving distance. Any (or all of them) could have had better and more lucrative opportunities for faithful employment than my job as a waiter, but instead I gave up on using my undergraduate degree after one rejection. Don't make this same mistake! Find ways to use your unique background to make more money than the average seminarian, if at all possible.

Juggling a part-time job with your studies and ministry commitments might not be your favorite thing to do, but graduating debt free will be a great feeling at the end! While it is not glamorous, we deeply respect our seminary students who are toughing it out at the local fast food or gas chain in order to keep earning income during their studies. The rhythm of a part-time job can often provide the positive stress you need to keep on top of your studies. And while it may be difficult to have less time with your spouse if you are married, most spouses will respect and appreciate how you are contributing financially and thinking ahead for your family.

You also need to think of your summers as your own personal capital campaign to earn as much money as possible. During the summer, most seminary students are inclined to go for a full-time ministry position. This is all well and good, but *only if* you are being paid a reasonable salary. If you know that the local McDonalds is paying more per hour than your church, talk to the church and ask them to raise the salary to match McDonalds' levels. If they won't, then you need to consider working part time at the church and full time at that McDonalds!

Whether you have a ministry job or another kind of job during the summer, we would suggest getting another job on top of that if you can, especially if you are a single student! Even delivering pizzas or waiting tables two nights a week can add a significant amount of income. If you have a summer ministry job, this can also help you to keep it to forty hours instead of letting it balloon to eighty hours the way ministry positions often do.

If you are one of those unfortunate people who can't seem to find a summer job—we don't believe you. It may stink that you didn't get that church or camp position for the summer, but that doesn't change the fact that a new school year is heading your way. Draw up a résumé and start dropping it off everywhere. If you can't find anything full time, take on several part-time positions. And on Saturdays, find elderly people who will pay you to mow their lawn. If your goal is to generate as much income as you can, you'll forget about what you hoped to be doing during the summer and focus on earning.

One of Ben's sage professors used to tell his students about the financial decisions he made in seminary that allowed him to take on the ministry calling he received. When he graduated he and his wife led a team to Ohio to plant a church. They made little to no money for a long time, and thus they needed the lessons of frugality they learned in seminary to equip them for the long, hard plant ahead. His part-time job during seminary was as a church janitor. This equipped him to be a church planter, since church planters often do everything—including cleaning bathrooms! Learn to work hard in seminary, because once you leave seminary, you will still have to work hard. Very few people leave seminary as the heir apparent to a financially sustainable church. Prepare yourself now by setting habits and disciplines that will bless you later!

CONCLUSION

Seminary students are not exactly entering a lucrative career path, so it is important that you work hard to keep your debt low. While most people intuitively recognize that debt is not a good thing, Christians along with the rest of society are lured into the debt lifestyle that modern culture preaches. Paying for something at the time of purchase rather than saving up over many years is now viewed as an antiquated method. But the debt-based economy is not God's view on money. God entrusts us with resources to steward and tells us that "the borrower is a slave of the lender" (Prov 22:7). We are called to be responsible stewards, and in the world of mounting student debt, seminary students can and should seek to be different. There are many ways to minimize your debt and be a better steward of the money you have either saved or borrowed. You know as well as we do the global reality—most of us are rich! Make the choice to embrace a lifestyle of biblical simplicity.

We want to reiterate—we were terrible at this. There were some periods during our studies where we followed some of these guidelines, but we weren't consistent. In the end, we simply did not commit ourselves to the task. The amount of debt you incur is largely determined by the choices you make. It may not be possible to be completely debt free, but by making wise decisions and frugal choices, you can cut your debt repayment by many years. Making these choices today will save you money and afford you choices tomorrow.

———— 🖋 ————

A Word to Spouses

We both have loving and encouraging wives who have supported us throughout our calling. Without them, we would not be where we are today; we recognize the importance of their role in our calling, our success, and our ministry. Danny met and married his wife while in seminary, and it made the experience so much better for him. Ben met his wife while in his doctoral work, and they got married halfway through his program. Without their encouragement and sacrifice along the way, we would have never made it! The same is true for your spouse who is pursuing their education. Although you are not sitting in the classes and doing the homework, it is very much a joint venture. Your spouse's calling is a team effort and it will take mutual sacrifice for this educational endeavor to be successful.

The following is a list of ideas we think will be helpful in the support of your spouse pursuing this degree.

Surviving and Thriving in Seminary

Following this list are three short stories about three very real seminary spouses. Read this appendix prayerfully as you consider your calling and your spouse's.

We do not know what your current circumstances are. It may be that the advice in this appendix is unhelpful given your situation. You may be a student yourself, you may have a high-demand job, or you may have an ailment that prevents you from some of the activities we recommend.

Whatever your situation, communication is always key. The truth is that marriages can often suffer during seminary, even to the point of divorce on occasion. No matter your circumstances, you and your spouse need to be proactive in defining boundaries, in staying connected, and in making hard decisions together.

1. Be Your Spouse's Cheerleader

Next to God, you are the most important person in your spouse's life. Your words and actions can make your spouse soar or sink. You have been given an incredible opportunity to be the cheerleader for your spouse and help them succeed, not just in seminary, but in any endeavor. Use this power to be a cheerleader for your spouse as they study. We firmly believe that words of affirmation demonstrate love and respect. Your words will encourage your spouse to press on in their pursuits.

2. Free up Your Spouse's Time

If you can sense that your spouse is genuinely working hard yet cannot seem to get everything done, ask yourself if there is anything you can do to free up some of their time. Are there chores that you can take over? Are there errands you can run instead? Can your spouse work while you cook supper? Can you take over the budgeting?

Can you make those phone calls and set up those appointments? While it may seem like you are now bearing the load for the entire household, remember that it is only for a period of time, and it will be an incredible gift to your spouse.

This will not work for all couples. After all, you also may have a very demanding job, or you yourself may be a student! The key is open and honest communication. You both need to be prepared to make sacrifices so that your goals are achieved without your relationship and life crumbling apart. You also need to help your spouse ask the hard questions. If your spouse can't seem to keep up, they may need to drop something significant: a course, a ministry at the church, a shift from work, etc. Sometimes your spouse will need you to tell them that making the hard choice to drop something is a good decision.

3. Contribute Financially

This is a no-brainer, particularly for couples that don't have children. But just to reiterate, make every effort to work to contribute as much financially as you can—after all, as a couple you share debt! And if you do have kids and stay at home, consider still whether there are things you can do to contribute financially. Offering to care for other children in your home is often the easiest way to earn some extra income, and some stay-at-home parents actually welcome the chance to get out of the house for a part-time job in the evenings.

4. Remind Your Spouse to Work

Help your spouse stick to their routine. We have outlined in this book a scheduling practice that, if followed, will help your spouse to thrive at seminary. Help your spouse stick to a routine by encouraging them to get up early, get to school or the library on time, and not work too late into the night. We have encouraged students to be their own taskmaster, but sometimes you'll need to remind your spouse of this!

There can often be times during a semester when students hit a wall and don't feel like doing anything. Hopefully your spouse will push through these times. A loving but firm voice reminding them to break through that wall and get on with it is sometimes necessary, and you are the perfect person to do it.

5. Remind Your Spouse to Rest

We both love what we do, and we could easily become workaholics if we weren't convinced and convicted about the necessity of rest and our primary calling to shepherd our family. Sometimes, however, we still get tunnel vision on a project and need the gentle reminder that there is a world beyond our books and projects.

There will be times when your spouse will need the reminder, gentle or firm, that it is okay to relax and rest. With so much work to do, endless deadlines, and a mountain of reading, it is easy for some students to become completely absorbed in their study. If your spouse follows the instructions we've given on time management, they will build rest into their weekly routine. But it would go a long way for you to remind your spouse of this as well.

6. Help Your Spouse Say No

You need to help your spouse say no on occasion in order to stay in alignment with the goals for seminary you have agreed on together. Some families have uprooted life to move to seminary for a season so they can return to a church or move overseas in pursuit of a calling. Some students are pursuing seminary on the side while working full time in a ministry or non-ministry field. Create an agreed-upon plan and then help your spouse to prioritize their schooling in a manner that matches your family goals.

Some (not all) people can be prone to over-committing themselves. This may be especially true of students who are also in ministry. You need to help your spouse jealously guard their time. Help your spouse say no when unnecessary requests for their time come in. When you can, run interference for your spouse to deflect these requests. In this increasingly busy world, one of the best productivity tips is to say no. Help your spouse to do that well.

7. Keep a Date Night

Because seminary will begin to consume your spouse's time, you will often find that those regular times to connect that you once had may diminish as they work hard on seminary studies. But your relationship certainly needs to be kept as a priority (don't worry—we let your spouse know this as well!).

No matter how busy your spouse is, keep that date night. You may not be able to go out for dinner, but you can go out for coffee or just for a long walk. Either way, *insist* on that time alone together to connect. One of Ben and his wife's favorite dates is to grab a cup of coffee and go to Barnes & Noble. She picks out a book she thinks he needs to read, and he in turn picks one out he thinks she needs to read. It has been a wonderful way for her to speak into his life and for him to encourage her to read some interesting (and *readable*) theology texts.

8. Remind Your Spouse of Their Calling

Your spouse may be prone to venting or complaining about all of the work, all of the reading, and so on. We all need someone to listen to us blow off some steam, and spouses usually are that person. After patiently listening, remind your spouse about their call by God and their desire to learn more.

Also, seminary students, and people in general, are often prone to sharing their frustrations, but not as prone to share their valuable insights. We encourage you to ask your spouse what they are learning and how they are being challenged. Help your spouse to focus on and verbalize the blessings of seminary, not just the frustrations. It is very easy for a student to lose sight of the big picture among the many details, so remind them.

9. Find a Close Circle of Friends

Seminary students often find camaraderie with their fellow students. Especially if you have moved, it is important for your own well-being to seek a good circle of friends too. Depending on the make-up of the seminary, this is usually more difficult for men whose wives are in seminary, but not impossible. We are created to live in community, and you will need a group of others besides your spouse to rely on and talk to. You will often find that seminary is demanding a lot of your spouse's time and you are not spending as much time together as you used to. Remember, this is only a season of life for you both. While you are in it, work hard to find someone who is in or has already gone through the same situation as you.

10. Pray for Your Spouse

We've saved the most important for last. Pray for your spouse. They have felt called by God to be in seminary. Perhaps it was a very specific call, or perhaps their call was just to make this first step into higher education. Either way, God has a purpose for your spouse in the building up of his kingdom. Pray every day for your spouse, and let them know it. Pray that they would learn as much as possible from the professors and readings. Pray your spouse they will manage and use their time wisely. Pray that your spouse would be a blessing to their seminary community. Your spouse will question things they had not questioned before, or change their opinion on certain subjects. Whole new worlds of information will come upon them. Pray that they would seek God's wisdom and truth through it all.

THREE STORIES

Ben's dissertation was a qualitative research study in which he interviewed fifteen seminary spouses about their non-student experiences in seminary. Specifically, he was interested in how they experienced spiritual transformation through their spouse's education. One of the things that surprised him the most about this study was that three of these spouses started seminary without a personal relationship with Christ. Each of the three had a different story and reason for their spiritual location, and in each of these stories the spouse, over the course of seminary, found their own relationship with Christ. We want to briefly share these stories, not because we think this is common for the seminary experience, but because both of us are committed to the good news of the gospel and its power to transform lives—in the lives of seminary students *and their spouses* (Rom 1:16–17).

Raised in church, but not saved. Ilise grew up in church, met her husband in the youth group, and the two got engaged after a missions trip. Her husband eventually became the youth pastor at their church. While he was in seminary, he had an assignment that required him to meet together with a small group and pray for an unreached people group. So after a revival at their church, Ilise and her husband joined with another couple and prayed for the lost. At home that night, as they were getting ready for bed, she was unusually quiet. Recounting her story, she said that her husband noticed her quietness and asked what was going on. She admitted that what was said at the revival and during their prayer time convicted her and she realized that she never had a personal relationship with Jesus. That very night, her husband led her to Christ in their bedroom.

Spirituality is not enough. Jocelyn's story was different, but she always considered herself "spiritual." Her first husband was an adamant atheist and squelched any interest she might have in spirituality. After her divorce, she met Jacob, who grew up as a Christian but had wandered from his faith. Shortly after their marriage he renewed his personal commitment to Christ and was called into ministry. At first she was excited because this was such a stark contrast from her first marriage; however, she eventually realized the extent of his faith and how his faith would impact her future, especially after he finished seminary and was called to pastor. So she started out on her own faith journey and came to the conclusion that being "spiritual" was not enough. As she started to study Scripture and explore faith on her own, she came to understand her own need for Christ's offer of salvation and the necessary response required.

A crisis of belief. Hailey grew up in the Mormon church, but her life was filled with several tragedies. She lost her father at a young age, as well as two of her siblings, and the Mormon church offered compassion, love, and doctrinal encouragement in a time when it was needed. As she grew, her zeal for her faith started to wane. Eventually she met and married Harold. He, like her, grew up committed to his Baptist faith, but his faith wandered in young adulthood. So when they got married, their different systems of faith didn't seem to matter. However, shortly into their marriage, he recognized his need and renewed his commitment to Christ. He was later called to ministry. Hailey eventually realized how their differing theologies were starting to impact their marriage. One day she came to the conclusion that she had three options: (1) continue in her marriage with differing theologies and get used to the conflict this caused, (2) get a divorce, or (3) figure out what she *actually* believed. This took her on a journey of inquiry. Meanwhile, Harold took his first pastorate at a small country church. It was during his first Easter sermon that the gospel finally clicked for her, and it was during his altar call that she stood, walked the aisle, and realized that salvation was not based on her doing, but on what Christ did—on the cross.

GOD'S STORY AND YOUR STORY

We tell these stories because we recognize that each of our students and each of their spouses come from a different background with a different story. The way you got to this book and this calling as a seminary spouse is unique. It is part of God's sovereign hand and the way that he has orchestrated your life. It is fun to share stories and hear about the varying paths that God uses to bring people to faith; however, we also wanted to tell these stories because we realize that not everyone comes to seminary as a follower of Jesus Christ, and because of this we want to take just a minute to explain to you who Jesus is and why we do what we do.

For those of you who know this story of Jesus, read on with a grateful heart and a prayerful spirit that the Lord might use these words to clearly communicate his good news to those who might be reading this paragraph with questions. For those of you with questions, read on for just a few minutes (and then talk to your spouse who presumably knows more about the story below).

First, the good news of Jesus starts sadly. Each of us was born into sin, and thus are separated from God at birth because of our sin. For those of you who are parents, ask, "Do I have to teach my children to do good or to do wrong?" If you've been a parent for any length of time you realize we *learn* how to do good; it is doing the bad that comes so naturally to all of us. This is because we were born into sin.

The Bible is God's story of how he has prepared a way to cover the chasm between him and us that is caused by our sin. In the Old Testament, God gave the people of Israel a series of laws, but these laws were to prove to God's people that every time they tried to perfectly follow the law, they failed. They could not *by their own strength* perfectly follow the law. So God, in his infinite wisdom, sent Jesus to live perfectly for us. He was then killed as a common criminal, but his blood provides an atonement, a covering for our sin. Jesus was our substitution and by his blood we have been declared righteous. This is what separates Christianity from other religious options. Only perfection warrants salvation, but we do not need to live the perfect life; Jesus has lived it for us so "that we might become the righteousness of God" (2 Cor 5:21). Jesus has given us his perfection! All we have to do is ask for it. All that is required is faith and repentance. First John 1:9 tells us that "if we confess our sins, he is faithful and just, so that he will forgive us our sins and will cleanse us from all unrighteousness."

It is out of gratefulness for what Jesus has done that we have committed our lives as his followers and teachers of his story. We hope and pray that each of you knows this story and commits your life to sharing it with the world. For those of you who don't know this story, please ask. Your spouse is the best starting point, but if you need more help, you can also find one of their professors—or contact us! We would love to introduce you to Jesus, the one who lived and died so that you might share in his perfection and be reconciled to God, forgiven from all your unrighteousness.

Acknowledgments

Danny would like to thank his wife and children for their continual love and support, as well as the students of Acadia Divinity College for whom the early forms of this material were originally written. Thanks are due also to the faculty and staff of Acadia Divinity College for their support and encouragement.

Ben would like to thank his wife Lerisa for her example, her love, and her wisdom. Our home would not be as wonderful of a place as it is without her! She graciously puts up with book ideas and the time needed to bring these ideas to fruition. She is a godly woman who is a blessing to her family! He would also like to thank all of those who have had a mentoring role in his life – especially those alluded to in this book, Bruce Forrest, Nathan Puzey, Keith Metzler, Ron Hawkins, Robert F. Dees, and Dave Earley.

Danny and **Ben** would like to thank Lexham Press for envisioning this project and helping to bring it to fruition. Brannon Ellis, Jesse Myers, and Elliot Ritzema are all an integral part of what has been set forth in this book. Their behind-the-scenes work may not be known to the readers, but their investment will lead to fruit in the lives of many seminarians. Thank you for your assistance and friendship!